The Slender Human Word focuses on Emerson as artist. Other scholars have dealt primarily with Emerson the thinker and have interpreted and elaborated his place in intellectual history. Emerson's significance, however, derives not only from his thought but also from his artistry as a writer, most especially from the way he employs imagery in his prose. This book examines the techniques he uses to transform his essays into prose-poems and thereby provides a much-needed, fresh look at Emerson the literary craftsman.

William J. Scheick finds that "Emerson's understanding of imagery lies at the core of his literary practice." For Emerson an artistic image is the product of the human will, and it represents the spontaneous transformation of unconscious instinct into conscious thought. His essays generally have an image at their center as an integrating or unifying device.

Emerson's use of imagery is extensive and skillfully interwoven throughout his best essays. He forms images into clusters or sequences, then layers and combines them into one master picture, a *hieroglyph*, governing each essay. Like hieroglyphs, his central images present a picture which fuses the natural and the spiritual realms, a figure visually communicating the secret relationship between these two realms. In Emerson's belief the careful use of imagery comprises the "true experience of the poet."

In this lucid study Scheick first examines Emerson's theories about imagery and his devising of the complex system applying those theories—the central hieroglyph. He then takes specific hieroglyphs and demonstrates how each unifies an essay and stimulates the reader at both a conscious and an unconscious level—deliberate planning by Emerson. He identifies individual images, image clusters or sequences, and the interrelatedness of all to the central image. The author's most minute observations are verified or amplified by Emerson's own words.

Scheick is convinced that Emerson the artist has not received the recognition he deserves, and his approach to supplying proof is both thorough and organized. But the author ultimately makes his point most convincingly by simulating Emerson's techniques. He has composed, in a sense, his own hieroglyph for this work, a controlled-yet-free composite of Emerson's shimmering imagery, a central picture which might be entitled Emerson the Artist.

William J. Scheick is associate professor of English at the University of Texas, Austin, where he also serves as editor of *Texas Studies in Literature and Language*. His wide-ranging work has appeared in numerous journals, and his books include *The Will and the Word: The Poetry of Edward Taylor; The Writings of Jonathan Edwards: Theme, Motif, and Style;* and *Seventeenth-Century American Poetry: A Reference Guide*.

The Slender Human Word

The Slender Human Word

EMERSON'S ARTISTRY IN PROSE

William J. Scheick

THE UNIVERSITY OF TENNESSEE PRESS

Knoxville

Library of Congress Cataloging in Publication Data

Scheick, William J.
  The slender human word.

  Includes bibliographical references and index.
    1.   Emerson, Ralph Waldo, 1803–1882—Style.
I.   Title.
PS1644.S3   814′.3   77–27020
ISBN 0–87049–222–5

For Marion and Jessica Holly

Contents

Preface

Over the years, as a student and as a teacher, my experience
with Ralph Waldo Emerson's writings proved discomforting
because they readily suited American literature courses designed to discuss intellectual history but always seemed somewhat intrusive in classes oriented toward literary analysis.
More than once I witnessed or heard of instructors who apologized for including Emerson in their assignments; sometimes
they simply apologized for Emerson.

Recent critical interest in Emerson's writings, however, has
focused less exclusively on his ideas or on the relation of his
work to his life and has increasingly emphasized his literary
techniques. Previous commentaries in general have complained
about an apparent lack of any logical or systematic presentation of thought in Emerson's essays. Ralph Rusk's opinion, expressed in his excellent biography of Emerson, is quite typical:
"Within each essay unity was only partial. Perhaps most passages could have been transferred from one paragraph to another or from one essay to another without harm. Only the
sentences were indisputably units." [1] This notion still survives,
perhaps most notably in Quentin Anderson's observation that
in Emerson's essays thought and artistry "played second fiddle
to the preacher's goals." [2]

But at present, as if in belated response to George Santa-

yana's and William James's general praise of Emerson's style,[3]
literary critics have amplified our understanding and appreciation of Emerson's prose by discussing various devices he substituted for more commonplace methods of exposition. Critics
have noted, for instance, how Emerson structured his essays
"in an ascending and widening spiral around a fixed center,
which is the major idea"; [4] how he was able, by means of analogy, to join the concrete to the ethereal; [5] how he avoided any
clear sense of beginning, middle, or end, thereby reflecting an
aspect of the universe as he saw it; [6] how he wrote in a "ba-
roque renascent style"; [7] how he "first wrote in a tradition domi-
nated by the rhetorical theory of the eighteenth century . . .
and gradually developed a very different theory, influenced by
writers of the romantic school of the late eighteenth and early
nineteenth centuries"; [8] and, in an especially fine study, how he
regulated rhythm, metaphor, and tone for conscious artistic
effect.[9] These and similar studies, such as the recognition of the
influence of Emerson's language on the audience response to
the Divinity School address [10] and of "a unity of attitude or
feeling" dominating each essay,[11] are significant because they
attempt to consider Emerson in accord with how he thought
of himself: as a literary artist as well as a thinker (L, I, 435).

In spite of these very useful studies, the degree to which
Emerson emphasized the function of the image has not been
recognized sufficiently. And yet, as my book is devoted to
demonstrating, Emerson's understanding of imagery lies at the
core of his literary practice, of his artistry in prose. It is Emerson the artist whom I hope to keep in immediate focus in this
book. Emerson the thinker is here too, as indeed of necessity
he must be; but, except for a discussion of Emerson's notion of
the dynamic will, I make no pretense to adding significantly to
current discussions of his thought. Others have done this task
excellently, and I call upon them as I need them. Emerson the
writer is my subject: his frequent development of an essay
around a central hieroglyph or picture created by numerous
related motifs, resulting not only in a unique internal structural principle but in a visionary experience for the sensitive

reader. I treat the essays as long prose poems requiring careful, even at times painstaking, exegesis to disclose the intricate, delicate, and beautiful precision of the artistic interplay of their language.

In Part 1, I speculate about the theory behind Emerson's art, particularly his notion of imagery and its relation to the art of ancient hieroglyphics and to the function of the human will. In Part 2, a number of essays are explicated. I have grouped certain essays in three of its four chapters in order to consider Emerson's development of a hieroglyph over the years —for his thought and artistry changed somewhat—and at the same time to examine each essay as a unique poetic expression.

The reader should be forewarned that, owing to Emerson's narrow range of images and to my critical procedure, an element of redundance is unavoidable. I beg the reader's indulgence, hoping that in most cases the repetition not only will allow for preservation of the essential artistic integrity of each essay under consideration but also will serve to make clearer some abstruse point or, at the very least, to convince by the sheer weight of evidence.

Nowhere do I mean to imply an exhaustive analysis of all the artistic particulars in any essay discussed. My aim is to locate the governing hieroglyph or emblematic imagery and to indicate the most striking features of its artistic development. There is, frankly, a limit to what I have seen and to how far my analytical prose can reach. Sometimes, albeit infrequently, I glimpsed strands of imagery which I never could quite relate to the central hieroglyph. Other times the strands were too redundant in terms of what Emerson had done previously or, in their minor function, too far beyond the strategies of structured critical commentary. Like brilliant poems, Emerson's best essays defy exhaustive analysis. They are *rich*, yielding upon each rereading still further displays of poetic genius. Like that of excellent poetry, the vision of Emerson's most accomplished essays always exceeds the sum of a critic's analytical particulars.

Although such limitations distress me—and I can see myself

years hence thinking back on this work and shaking my head in disbelief that there was so much I did not see or say—this experience of an expanding yet elusive horizon of insight is wholly in accord with Emerson's thought and artistic practice. Such is my consolation, at least for the time being.

Abbreviations

FOR WORKS BY EMERSON

Citations of works by Ralph Waldo Emerson are inserted in parentheses directly into the text, immediately following a quotation or reference. Each citation can be identified by the code reference below, with its appropriate volume number and page number.

CW   *The Collected Works of Ralph Waldo Emerson: Volume I, Nature, Addresses, and Lectures*, ed. Robert E. Spiller and Alfred R. Ferguson. Cambridge: Harvard Univ. Press, 1971.

EL   *The Early Lectures of Ralph Waldo Emerson*, three volumes. *Volume I, 1833–1836*, ed. Stephen E. Whicher and Robert E. Spiller (1959). *Volume II, 1836–1838*, ed. Stephen E. Whicher, Robert E. Spiller, and Wallace E. Williams (1964). *Volume III, 1838–1842*, ed. Robert E. Spiller and Wallace E. Williams (1972). Cambridge: Harvard Univ. Press.

JMN   *The Journals and Miscellaneous Notebooks of Ralph Waldo Emerson*, 11 volumes. *Volume I, 1819–1822*, ed. William H. Gilman, Alfred R. Ferguson,

George P. Clark, and Merrell R. Davis (1960).
Volume II, 1822–1826, ed. William H. Gilman, Alfred R. Ferguson, and Merrell R. Davis (1961).
Volume III, 1826–1832, ed. William H. Gilman and
Alfred R. Ferguson (1963). *Volume IV, 1832–1834,*
ed. Alfred R. Ferguson (1964). *Volume V, 1835–
1838,* ed. Merton M. Sealts, Jr. (1965). *Volume VI,
1824–1838,* ed. Ralph H. Orth (1966). *Volume VII,
1838–1842,* ed. A. W. Plumstead and Harrison Hay-
ford (1969). *Volume VIII, 1841–1843,* ed. William H. Gilman and J. E. Parsons (1970). *Volume
IX, 1843–1847,* ed. Ralph H. Orth and Alfred R.
Ferguson (1971). *Volume X, 1847–1848,* ed. Merton M. Sealts, Jr. (1973). *Volume XI, 1848–1851,*
ed. A. W. Plumstead and William H. Gilman
(1975). Cambridge: Harvard Univ. Press.

L   *The Letters of Ralph Waldo Emerson,* six volumes, ed.
Ralph L. Rusk. New York: Columbia Univ. Press,
1939.

W   *The Complete Works of Ralph Waldo Emerson* ("Cen-
tenary Edition"), 12 volumes, ed. Edward Waldo
Emerson. Boston: Houghton Mifflin, 1903–1904.

Part 1: *Theory*

I

Sea Shells
Wet Upon the Beach

In a journal entry for 1836, Emerson noted: "I cannot hear a sermon without being struck by the fact that amid drowsy series of sentences what a sensation a historical fact, a biographical name, a sharply objective illustration makes!" (JMN, V, 197). As his notions about art developed over the years, Emerson increasingly accentuated the importance of the image. A good writer, he eventually concluded, must "put the argument into a concrete shape, into an image,—some hard phrase, round and solid as a ball" (W, VII, 90). Since the careful use of imagery comprises the "true experience of the poet," it is not surprising that late in life Emerson made the following remark about his own work: "I had rather have a good symbol of my thought, or a good analogy, than the suffrage of Kant or Plato. If you agree with me, or if Locke or Montesquieu agree, I may yet be wrong; but if the elm-tree thinks the same thing, if running water, if burning coal, if crystals, if alkalies, in their several fashions say what I say, it must be true" (W, VIII, 32, 13). Emerson early had maintained that the wise man fastens words to visible things and that the resultant "picturesque language is at once a commanding certificate that he who employs it, is a man in alliance with truth and God" (CW, I, 20).

To some extent this trust in the image influenced Emerson's practice of sifting through his journals for material, a procedure which doubtless contributed to the seemingly fragmentary quality of many essays. Beyond question he must have judged a particular passage appropriate for inclusion chiefly in terms of whether it suited the topic of a lecture or essay. At times, however, subject matter was not a sole criterion. Occasionally Emerson's editing reveals the deletion of passages which are relevant to his theme and the addition of others which fail to contribute very satisfactorily to the overall argument of an essay.

I am not suggesting that Emerson lacked control in his revisions; ample evidence testifies to the contrary.[1] I mean that the presence of a certain image or phrase in a journal entry often figured in Emerson's decision to include it. Upon reconsideration, Emerson observed, "a man may find his words mean more than he thought when he uttered them & be glad to employ them again in a new sense"; sometimes "what I write whilst I write it seems the most natural thing in the world[,] but yesterday I saw only a dreary vacuity in this very direction in which I now see so much" (JMN, V, 409; VII, 293). These remarks indicate, among other matters, that a latent image in yesterday's journal may suddenly participate in a more striking future revelation of the reality behind all symbols. For the soul, which transcribes this revelation, "is progressive, it never quite repeats itself, but in every act attempts the production of a new and fairer whole" (W, II, 351). In certain instances Emerson's standard for selecting a notebook entry was set by how well an image in it contributed to the "fairer whole" of the imagistic structure of the particular essay.

Imagery and the Will

Emerson's emphasis on imagery derived in part from personal experience with its centrality in the process of thought. "I never take a step in thought," he noted in his journal in 1835, "without some material symbol of my proposition figuring itself incipiently at the same time" (JMN, V, 77). Later he similarly indicated that "a man conversing in earnest, if he watch his intellectual processes, will find that a material image, more or less luminous, arises in his mind, contemporaneous with every thought" (CW, I, 20). Emerson based these generalizations on his complex notion of the interaction in man between instinct, will, and thought. He believed that "communication with absolute truth" is achieved through "thought and instinct" (W, VII, 37). These comprise the polarities, as it were, of man's mental process, and between them lies the will.[2]

Although Emerson apparently preferred not to speak of the will too specifically, he could not avoid, any more than could his Puritan ancestors, using the term in a manner suggesting its separateness as a unique faculty; nor did he always escape the commonplace negative sense of the will as manifesting willfulness or human perversity. For him, however, the word *will* generally refers to the mysterious dynamic interaction between instinct and thought, a concept discussed in the next chapter.

Because he regarded an image as incipient to and nearly simultaneous with thought, then that image is affiliated with the point of transformation between instinct and thought. This notion is evident in the assertion that "the active power seizes instantly the fit image, as the word of its momentary thought" (W, II, 334). The active power is the will, the source of an image which Logos-like unites divine instinct and human thought. That Emerson wished to preserve a sense of simultaneity in this instantaneous union explains why in the entry from his notebook and in the passage from *Nature* (his first published book, 1836) he refers to the production of this image as occurring "at the same time" or "contemporaneous with every thought"; like the Logos, in its incarnation as Christ (an idea in which Emerson did not believe but was ready to appropriate), the divine and earthly aspects of the will's spontaneous image cannot be meaningfully considered separately. The spontaneous moment of interaction defines the very nature of the will and of its Logos-like image. Literary art, then, with its concern with imagery—imagery is for Emerson the true experience of the poet (W, VIII, 32)—represents the result of nature working "through the will of a man" (CW, I, 17).[3]

The feature of the will known as human instinct derives, according to Emerson, from the divinity that dwells deep within man's unconscious resources. A force beyond human control, it generates spontaneous moments wherein it is transformed into thought or consciousness. Because for him this impulse is divine in origin, Emerson readily trusted in the appropriateness of the unpremeditated Logos-like image engendered by the dynamic interaction between instinct and thought. Consider, for example, his observation, made some time in 1845 or 1846, about the Reverend Edward Taylor:

> His sovereign security results from a certain renunciation &
> abandonment. He runs for luck, & by readiness to say
> everything[,] good & bad, says the best things. Then a new
> will & understanding organize themselves in this new sphere
> of no-will & no-understanding, and as fishermen use a certain
> discretion within their luck, to find a good fishing-ground,
> or the berry women to gather quantities of whortleberries, so
> he knows his topics, & his unwritten briefs, and where the
> profusion of words & images will likeliest recur. With all his
> volleys of epithets & imagery, he will ever & anon hit the
> white.   (JMN, IX, 259)

Emerson respected Taylor's reliance upon instinct to yield spontaneously an image which would convey his thought clearly. To engender imagery in this fashion is, for Emerson, the essence of art: "The conscious utterance of thought, by speech or action, to any end, is Art" (W, VII, 38). That is, art results from the interaction between unconscious instinct and conscious thought: "Art is the spirit's voluntary use and combination of things to serve its end. The Will distinguishes it as spiritual action" (W, VII, 39). Relying on a traditional Christian notion of the will (albeit with Hegelian overtones) as the abode of the Holy Spirit and as the originating center of thought, word, and deed,[4] Emerson readily refers to art, the expression of the will's dynamic union of instinct and thought, as "the spirit creative" (W, VII, 39). The artist, it follows, "must work in the spirit in which we conceive a prophet to speak, or an angel of the Lord to act" (W, VII, 48).

As a product of the artist's will, in the sense of the inter-

action between instinct and thought, the image communicates
to the will of the audience.[5] "A figurative statement arrests attention, and is remembered and repeated. . . . Mark the
delight of an audience in an image" (W, VIII, 12), Emerson
observes, indicating here as elsewhere in his writings that
artistic vision engenders vision in others. Ideally the reader
experiences the very process of dynamic interaction between
instinct and thought which produced the delightful striking
image. "We are dazzled at first by new words and brilliancy of
color, which occupy the fancy and deceive the judgment. But
all this is easily forgotten. Later, the thought, the happy image
which expressed it and which was the true experience of the
poet, recurs to mind, and sends me back in search of the book"
(W, VIII, 32). The image, the union of instinct and thought,
stimulates the audience's own interaction between instinct
and thought.[6] This principle of the dynamic animation of the
audience's will is in part what Emerson has in mind when he
explains that "nothing so works on the human mind, barbarous
or civil, as a trope. Condense some daily experience into a
glowing symbol, and an audience is electrified" (W, VII, 90).
"The symbol always stimulates" (JMN, IX, 348); art proves
successful only "when it astonishes and fires us with new en-
deavors after the unattainable" (W, II, 180). The unattainable
is ultimate truth, which always recedes even as man steadily
approaches it through the generation of ever-new thoughts.
The electrifying image (like its adjuncts, the provocative epi-
gram and paradox) remains at once accessible and elusive; but
it always stimulates interaction of instinct and thought.

In this manner, mankind intellectually advances in a spiral
ascent. Each subsequent thought is not accreted; rather mankind advances, as does the soul of each of its members, in terms
of a metamorphosis (W, II, 274) akin to St. Paul's observation
about the flesh: "It is sown a natural body; it is raised a spiritual
body" (EL, I, 289). The electrifying image releases an audience from the confines of present thought by arousing its will
into producing a still more elevated image; "As the bird alights
on the bough, then plunges into the air again, so the thoughts

of God pause for a moment in any form" (W, VIII, 15). Each revelation "is progressive, it never quite repeats itself, but in every act attempts the production of a new and fairer whole" (W, II, 351). This sense of the reader or hearer experiencing the very process which led the artist to produce his electrifying image underlies the statement that "there is then creative reading, as well as creative writing" (CW, I, 58).

Emerson's notion that the active power or will seizes the fit image as the word of its momentary thought does not merely apply to individual sentences. That he fashioned impressive epigrammatic sentences which time and again pivot on a striking image is amply attested to by the fact that many survive today as aphorisms. But the brilliant sentence is not Emerson's principal achievement; the sentence was important to him only in terms of how it contributed to the aesthetic unity of an entire essay, a unity based on an underlying picture coordinating all the imagery of individual sentences. In other words, each essay functions in its entirety as if it were a fable, a proverb, or an emblem.

In Emerson's opinion, a fable is merely an image magnified. It too derives from the dynamic encounter of instinct and thought: "fable has in it somewhat divine. It came from thought above the will of the writer" and emanates from "his constitution and not from his too active invention" (W, II, 108). Like an image, which it represents in large, the fable symbolizes or pictures truth, "a moral that is true to the core of the world" (JMN, VII, 397), derived from the transforming power of some artist's essentially passive yet active will. Similarly, "every common proverb is only one of [the] facts in nature used as a picture or parable of a more extensive truth" (EL, I, 25); "the proverbs of nations, consist usually of a natural fact, selected as a picture or parable of a moral truth" (CW, I, 22).[7] In short, Emerson speaks of fables and proverbs as if they were emblems. As he makes clear in *Nature*, every word is emblematic of some natural fact, and every natural fact is in turn emblematic of some spiritual truth (CW, I, 17). Man's "tuition is through emblems" (W, VI, 318); "all poets, orators,

& philosophers, have been those who could most sharply see & most happily present emblems, parables, figures. Good writing & brilliant conversation are perpetual allegories" (JMN, V, 63).

Each essay, if it is to be an artistic expression, must become an allegory, fable, parable, proverb, or emblem—terms which, as the preceding quotations indicate, Emerson often used interchangeably and fairly consistently. This means that, as with the individual images incorporated in it, each essay should be a pictorial expression resulting from Emerson's transforming will, from the dynamic interaction between his unconscious instinct and his conscious thought. In its entirety each essay should present "a material image, more or less luminous" contemporaneous with the thought it conveys.

Like that of Reverend Edward Taylor, Emerson's artistry aims to combine inspiration (or a certain unconscious wildness) with thought (or a certain conscious restraint), an idea reflected as well in Thoreau's view of his beanfield as the link between wildness and cultivation. On October 5, 1835, Emerson wrote in his journal: "I like that poetry which without aiming to be allegorical, is so. Which sticking close to its subject & that perhaps trivial can yet be applied to the life of man & the government of God & be found to hold" (JMN, V, 88). The ordinary image, symbol, or allegory at the heart of an essay should be divine in origin—that is, it ought to arise spontaneously from the instinct—but finally it should express both the wildness of instinct and the restraint of thought. "A man's *style* is his intellectual Voice only in part under his controul" (JMN, III, 26); as this remark implies, the artist does exercise some limited control subsequent to the creative impulse.

In compliance with this notion, Emerson tried to avoid attributing arbitrary meanings and associations to the central emblem of each essay; rather he endeavored to read the natural symbol as fundamentally as his New England ancestors approached Scripture. For him, a natural image possesses inherent emblematic meanings and associations quite independent of the conscious inventiveness of the artist, though the artist engages his mind in perceiving these intuitive meanings.

The Mysterious Hieroglyph

Hieroglyph is the term I shall use throughout this study to designate this natural image controlling and unifying each essay. It is a term Emerson used occasionally which has the added advantage of suggesting more accurately the complex features of his conception of a central image than do the words *allegory, symbol, parable, fable,* and *emblem*—all roughly synonymous with *hieroglyph* to Emerson.[8]

Emerson's appreciation of the hieroglyph is founded on his concept of the word, the creation of the image-producing will, as a picture of some natural fact. In his opinion "language is fossil poetry," the "deadest word . . . once a brilliant picture": "As the limestone of the continent consists of infinite masses of the shells of animalcules, so language is made up of images or tropes, which now, in their secondary use, have long ceased to remind us of their poetic origin" (W, III, 22).

√ In *Nature* he more simply states that "as we go back in history, language becomes more picturesque, until its infancy, when it is all poetry"; for every word, "if traced to its root, is found to be borrowed from some material appearance" (CW, I, 18–19). Emerson believed that the letters of the alphabet probably could not be compared directly to the figures of Egyptian hieroglyphics, but that words perform similarly because, like hieroglyphics, they convey a picture or image of expressed thought, an emblem bearing intrinsic symbolic implications not apparent to the weak perception of the average person.

Many of Emerson's contemporaries, as John Irwin has remarked,[9] expressed a keen interest in Egyptian hieroglyphics. During the early nineteenth century, America underwent an Egyptian revival stimulated by the arrival of Egyptian antiquities, which influenced architectural style and scholarly commentary. It is not surprising, then, that in *The Narrative of Arthur Gordon Pym* (1838) Poe should have his protagonists encounter mysterious hieroglyphical configurations; that in *The Scarlet Letter* (1850) Hawthorne should refer to Pearl as a living hieroglyph; that in *Walden* (1854) Thoreau should wonder whether someone like Champollion will decipher the hieroglyphics of nature; or that in *Moby-Dick* (1851) Melville should speak of Queequeg's tatooing, Ahab's marked brow, and the whale's sides as hieroglyphical.

Emerson's interest in hieroglyphics, which in one place he refers to as "Egyptian emblems" (JMN, IX, 348), was fairly extensive. The word *hieroglyph* appears frequently in his writings in contexts which implicitly and explicitly indicate the Egyptian prototype. In an early lecture entitled "The Naturalist" (1834), for instance, he observed: "As men have been fingering the characters that are carved on the Egyptian remains these thousand years, sure that they mean something if we could only find out the cipher, so for a much longer period men have been groping at the hieroglyphics of Nature to find out the cipher, assured that they mean something, assured that we shall understand ourselves better for what we shall read in the sea and the land and the sky" (EL, I, 78). In *Nature* he similarly remarked, "Every man's condition is a solution in hieroglyphic to those inquiries he would put" (CW, I, 7). Elsewhere he spoke of the hieroglyphic significance of kings (CW, II, 63), of Swedenborg's ability to read the world as "a grammar of hieroglyphs" (CW, IV, 142), and of nature as the poet's hieroglyphic (CW, VIII, 65).

Moreover, on October 12, 1838, Emerson asked Margaret Fuller whether she had read a long essay on Chinese characters and Egyptian hieroglyphics which appeared in the *Foreign Quarterly Review* (L, II, 168).[10] Commenting on Peter L. DuPonceau's *A Dissertation on the Nature and Character of the Chinese System of Writing,* the anonymous author of this article discussed the two major interpretations of how Chinese characters and Egyptian hieroglyphics functioned. Whereas DuPonceau argued that Chinese characters represent words and express ideas through these words, the reviewer defended the position that Chinese writing acts *vi propria,* presenting ideas directly to the mind through the eye: "Chinese characters half-picture the objects on the retina: and those characters consequently may be considered as holding a power, inferior indeed to the reality, but superior to the relation of it in words; they are a conventional picturesque." [11] Several other concerns were raised in the review, including both repudiation of the notion that the origin of letters is traceable to a system of picture writing and explanation of Egyptian hieroglyphics as a form of priestly writing.

It would be specious to conclude that this review essay sparked Emerson into some new direction of thought about his own artistic practice. I would even hesitate to say that it crystallized the idea of using a central hieroglyph as a picture organizing all the parts of an essay, even though Emerson significantly developed this technique after writing "The American Scholar," delivered a year before publication of this review. Emerson's mention of the article does indicate his interest in the subject, the degree to which he was exposed to the complex issues involved, and the value he placed on the article. Some speculation about the relation between the ideas in the review and Emerson's artistic practice is warranted.

In conjunction with the influence of the *Foreign Quarterly Review* essay, Sir John Gardner Wilkinson, Jean François Champollion, Edward Everett, and Sampson Reed, Emerson was exposed to ideas about Egyptian hieroglyphics from several other sources.

In *The Enneads,* for example, Plotinus speaks of "the wise of Egypt," who "indicated the truth where, in their effort towards philosophical statement, they left aside the writing-forms that take in the detail of words and sentences—those characters that represent sounds and convey the propositions of reasoning—and drew pictures instead, engraving in the temple-inscriptions a separate image for every separate item: thus they exhibited the absence of discursiveness in the Intellectual Realm" (V, 8, 6).[12] Swedenborg also indicates that the hieroglyphics of Egypt reveal a knowledge of the correspondence between the material and spiritual realms.[13] Nor in this regard should one overlook the influence on Emerson of the English religious poets of the seventeenth century.[14] In *Emblems,*

Quarles writes: "Before the knowledge of letters God was known by *Hieroglyphicks:* And, indeed, what are the Heavens, the Earth, nay every Creature, but *Hieroglyphicks* and *Emblems* of His Glory?" [15] Later, in his prefatory remarks to *Hieroglyphikes of the Life of Man,* Quarles explains: "If you are satisfied with my *Emblems,* I here set before you a second service. It is an Ægyptian dish, drest on the English fashion." [16] George Herbert, perhaps Emerson's favorite among the seventeenth-century poets of whom he was so fond, advanced this hieroglyphic tradition through the elaborate analogies and sometimes interesting typography of his brilliant poetry. Emerson observed of Herbert that he is "not content with the obvious properties of natural objects but delights in discovering abstruser relations between them and the subject of his thought" (EL, I, 349). It is interesting to note that, like Emerson, both Quarles and Herbert, among others of their time, did not distinguish among the terms *hieroglyph, emblem, analogy,* or *parable.* [17]

By hieroglyph Emerson means what his sources mean, a picture fusing material and spiritual realms, a figure or image visually communicating this secret symbolic relationship. Hieroglyph does not denote an arbitrary significance attributed to a symbol or emblem by a particular artist; rather it implies an intrinsic universal sign-value, a hidden self-explanatory moral or allegory, which the true artist intuits. The difference between these two approaches to art relates to the Kantian distinction between the Understanding and the Reason, which Emerson learned from Coleridge and others. [18] The Understanding, the lower function of the human mind concerned with divisibility and measurement, determines the construction of logical and arbitrary relationships: "the Usurping Understanding[,] the lieutenant of Reason, his hired man, the moment the Master is gone steps into his place[;] this usher commands, sets himself to finish what He [the Master] was doing, but instantly proceeds with his own dwarf Architecture . . . until presently for a moment Reason returns & the slave obeys" (JMN, V, 181). Arbitrary symbols are the "dwarf Architecture" of the Understanding, whereas the intuitive perception of the Reason, the higher function of the human mind, discerns the intrinsic architectonic of the natural emblem.

As the passage from Emerson's journal cited in the preceding paragraph indicates, Reason returns "for a moment"; the artist attains only a fleeting glimpse of the intrinsic meaning of the symbol. Furthermore, his vision is never complete. Emerson maintained that emblems of nature, like Egyptian hieroglyphics, always retain their essentially mysterious character and thus never emerge fully into the realm of conscious thought. In an early lecture he had emphasized that "the universe is prevaded with *secret analogies* that tie together its remotest parts," and it was because George Herbert read this "*riddle* of the world with a poet's eye" that Emerson admired his work (EL, III, 158; I, 353; italics added). Similarly Emerson wrote in his journal: "The deepest pleasure comes I think from the occult belief that an unknown meaning & consequence lurk in the common every day facts & as this panoramic or pictorial beauty can arise from it, so can a solid wisdom when the Idea shall be seen as such which binds these gay shadows together" (JMN, V, 212). The hieroglyphics of nature, like those of the Egyptians, retain a mysterious occult meaning, even as Pythagoras (another of Emerson's favorite authors) had argued concerning the secret doctrine of numbers (a doctrine related, at least for Plutarch—in "Of Isis and Osiris"—and for Emerson, to that of the hieroglyph).

This concept of the ultimate elusiveness of nature's hieroglyphics underlies Emerson's questions recorded in an 1836 journal entry: "Will any say that the Meaning of the world is exhausted when he sees the allegory of a single natural process?" (JMN, V, 185); and "Have you quite found out why every natural form, the acorn, the claw, the pine cone, the egg, the palm, and every tree & every leaf should be beautiful?" (JMN, V, 185). The self-explanatory yet always mysterious hieroglyphics of nature are epitomized for Emerson in the stars, one of nature's finest emblems:

> We cannot learn the cipher
> That's writ upon our cell;
> Stars taunt us by a mystery
> Which we could never spell.
> ("The World-Soul," W, IX, 17)

The stars "awaken a certain reverence, because though always present, they are always inaccessible"; "all natural objects make a kindred impression, when the mind is open to their influence" (CW, I, 9).

The Hieroglyph and the Emersonian Artist

For Emerson, the poet, above all others, possesses a mind most frequently open to the influence of nature's hieroglyphics and consequently he is destined to communicate his perception. Emerson associated the role of the poet with that of the priest; for, among other factors, in his time traditions pertaining to Egyptian hieroglyphics emphasized that the ancient priest class was centrally involved in the mystery of hieroglyphics.

In the *Foreign Quarterly Review*, for instance, the author of the article on DuPonceau's book speaks of the reluctance of the "priestly scribes to simplify their system for the vulgar," resulting in pictures designed for the purposes of mystification and concealment.[19] Similarly Giovanni Pico della Mirandola, whose name appears frequently in Emerson's journals, indicates that priests of pagan religions used hieroglyphics to conceal revelations; their myths and fables were designed to distract the attention of the multitude and thereby protect divine secrets from profanation.[20] *Iamblichus on the Mysteries of the Egyptians, Chaldeans, and Assyrians*, of which Emerson owned both a Latin edition (1556) and the Thomas Taylor translation (1821),[21] likewise refers to the Egyptian priests' imitative use of *synthemata* or inexplicable theurgic signs and symbols (II. xi; VII. i in Taylor's translation); and Plutarch in "Of Isis and Osiris" (from which Emerson cites on numerous occasions in his journals and essays) not only reveals the meaning of several

hieroglyphs but specifically emphasizes the Egyptian priests'
sense of obligation "to conceal the greater part [of their beliefs]
in tales and romantic relations, containing dark hints and re-
semblances of truth." [22]

The average person looking at a hieroglyph or hearing a
fable merely comprehends the surface level of the revelation
although that very level intrinsically reveals to the initiate still
deeper layers or dimensions of meaning and insight. This image
or allegory discloses even as it conceals profound mysteries,
but only the educated eyes of the priests can penetrate its
underlying spiritual significance.

Emerson emphasized that certain individuals, intuitively
perceiving more than the majority, penetrate deeply into the
mysteries of nature's hieroglyphics: "the office of the Poet is to
perceive and use . . . analogies. He converts the solid globe,
the land, the sea, the air, the sun, the animals into symbols of
thought. He makes the outward creation subordinate and
merely a convenient alphabet to express thoughts and emo-
tions" (EL, I, 291). Emerson did not, however, believe that
contemporary poet-priests need to protect the symbols or
mystica dogmata from the vulgar mind. To be sure, God "communicates with us by hints, omens, influence and dark resem-
blances in objects lying all around us" (W, VIII, 12); but He
does so in this manner because, as both Dionysius the Areopagite and Coleridge argued,[23] truth cannot be perceived by man
except through a poetic veil. Even as early as 1824, Emerson
maintained that the mind cannot discern the truth unless the
latter is symbolically represented:

> Metaphysicians are mortified to find how entirely the whole
> materials of understanding are derived from sense. No man is
> understood who speculates on mind or character until he
> borrows the emphatic specific imagery of Sense. A mourner
> will try in vain to explain the extent of his bereavement better
> than to say a *chasm* is opened in society. I fear the progress
> of Metaphys[ical] philosophy may be found to consist in
> nothing else than the progressive introduction of apposite
> metaphors. Thus the Platonists congratulated themselves for

ages upon their knowing that Mind was a dark chamber
whereon ideas like shadows were painted.

(JMN, II, 224–25)

Although his imagery functions like "the sublime symbols in
which the sages of the most ancient world were accustomed to
clothe their reverent theology" (EL, II, 353), for Emerson,
finally, there is no real distinction between poetic priest and
audience; the former merely represents what the latter can
become because "all men are poets, though in a less degree"
(EL, I, 228). Everyone, in Emerson's view, is a potential initiate into the mysteries of nature's hieroglyphics. Moreover,
unlike Giovanni Pico della Mirandola, Emerson was certain
that those mysteries could be revealed in plain language because everyday words—bear in mind here his fondness for the
vernacular and for folk idioms—are merely pictures of nature's
pictures or hieroglyphics divulging spiritual truth.

Like the priests of pagan mysteries, however, Emerson realized that the minds of most are not prepared to see beneath
the superficial level of fable, proverb, allegory, or emblem.
Even the poet-priest only partially penetrates the hieroglyphics
of nature; for, although always present, they remain ultimately
inaccessible. Appropriately Emerson notes how the priestly expression of these symbols in, say, the fables or parables of Plato
and Jesus "is at once exoteric & esoteric" (JMN, V, 31).[24] In
this sense the artist's image performs similarly to the Egyptian
hieroglyphic. But, unlike the Egyptian literati, Emerson's poet-
priest tries less to conceal than to awaken the divinity within
each member of his audience so that each may glimpse the
spiritual mysteries beneath the superficial, albeit organic, features of his fable.

A literary artist, according to Emerson, can prepare an audience for the electrifying effect of the "glowing symbol" by
using paradox.[25] Doubtless Emerson's sense of the importance
of paradox as an initiatory device explains why he decided to
commence *Poems* (1846) with "The Sphinx." (The title of this
poem reinforces our remarks about the influence on Emerson
of ancient Egyptian priests and their art—sphinxes were placed

before temples to admonish priests against revealing sacred secret symbols to the profane.) [26] Because the shock of paradox reveals yet conceals by suggesting more than what seems to be said, it is a most suitable means of stimulating audience receptivity. In one instance Emerson explained: "in our lapsed estate, resting, not advancing, resisting, not coöperating with the divine expansion, this growth comes by shocks" (W, II, 125). Like Giovanni Pico della Mirandola and George Herbert, among others, Emerson used riddles and epigrammatic remarks which convey mental jolts, comments which seem to jut forward into a consciousness that retreats before full awareness has occurred. Paradox communicates a foretaste of the hieroglyphic experience and thereby disposes an audience to keener alertness toward perceiving the emblematic mystery underlying an essay as a whole. Paradox, like the hieroglyph it serves, functions similarly to one of Goethe's poems, which "awakens the reader's invention . . . by the wild freedom of the design, and by the unceasing succession of brisk shocks of surprise" (W, II, 34).[27]

Such revelation is progressive. Each new insight prepares for the next, as the starlike hieroglyph evades final elucidation. Somewhat ahead of the rest of mankind, the poet-priest discovers each new level of perception; every subsequent expression of nature's hieroglyphics in his own words (which are merely pictures of those natural objects or symbols) must divulge this new insight. The images or objects of nature remain constant for the poet-priest, but "he makes the same objects exponents of his new thought" (W, III, 34). The artist's function is to divulge these ever-elusive yet self-revealing images of nature, to entice his audience into new vistas of insight concerning the mysteries of these symbols. He stimulates each person's instinct so that, through the dynamics of the will, it transforms into new thought. In this manner mankind advances or matures steadily as it continues to approach, though never attains, the vanishing point of the ultimate significance of nature's hieroglyphics.

Whenever the genuine artist uses nature's symbols as "a

convenient alphabet," his art functions in a fashion similar to Chinese characters and Egyptian hieroglyphics. Emerson was certain that "a good symbol is the best argument, and is a missionary to persuade thousands" (W, VIII, 13). "The poet who shall use Nature as his hieroglyphic," he concluded, cannot help but "have an adequate message to convey thereby" (W, VIII, 65). This was Emerson's aim. He selected some image pertaining to nature, man, or both and reflected it in the essay as a whole, not merely in individual words, sentences, or proverbs.

His best essays present a composite picture, a stable image underlying the foreground of flowing sentences and organizing lesser but related images of central words in these sentences. Each essay becomes a painting, its words and sentences strokes of the artist's brush. "Poets & painters ever walk abreast," Emerson wrote in 1834, reflecting his belief, doubtless to some degree influenced by the emblematic tradition of the seventeenth century, in the interrelatedness of poetry and painting (JMN, IV, 362); "painting was called 'silent poetry,' and poetry 'speaking painting,'" he explained a few years later, "the laws of each art are convertible into the laws of every other" (EL, II, 51). Commenting on an unnamed author, probably Wordsworth, Emerson similarly reflected: "Almost every moral line in his book might be framed like a picture, or graven in a temple porch, & would gain & not lose by being pondered" (JMN, IV, 431).

Like the painter, the literary artist "both draws well & colors at the same time" (JMN, VIII, 180), meaning that he produces not only the distinct lines of sentence units but also a more general effect. In 1844, Emerson observed: "In modern sculpture & picture & poetry, the beauty is miscellaneous, the artist works here & there & at all points, adding and adding, instead of developing the unit of his thought" (JMN, IX, 80). Consistent with his notion of the inexhaustibleness of the artist's imagery deriving from nature's mysterious hieroglyphics, Emerson concluded that no artist should limit his thought in terms of some narrow unit. As a result, discursive prose, with its emphasis on logical compartmentalization or units of development, proves inadequate to the literary artist. The artist needs to compose a prose medium which, like a good painting, communicates a stable effect amidst the swirl of particulars, to fashion a unified picture comprised of miscellaneous sentences. For Emerson, this picture is a hieroglyph, a self-revealing yet elusive image subliminally divulging to the inner eye of Reason its inherent symbolic truth. The uninitiated, utilizing only the Understanding, seize upon this or that sentence, detail, or proverb; though they perceive parts rather than the whole, even they cannot help but receive something of the impression conveyed. Like the hieroglyph at its core, each of Emerson's best essays conceals even as it reveals; it is never so literal as to be readily accessible to the conscious mind and never so transcendent as to evade intuitive perception completely.

The Hieroglyph in Emerson's Essays

Hieroglyphs underlying essays discussed in the following chapters were meant to be glimpsed. They appeal to Reason, not to the Understanding. They operate more subtly than do the hieroglyphs of George Herbert's "Man" and "The Pulley," two of Emerson's favorite poems, and more successfully than do the painterly effects of the Reverend Edward Taylor's elusive miscellaneous imagery, about which Emerson wrote:

> A creature of instinct, his colors are all opaline & doves'-neck-lustres & can only be seen at a distance. Examine them & they disappear. If you see the ignis fatuus in a swamp, & go to the place, the light vanishes; if you retire to the spot whereon you stood, it reappears. So with Taylor's muse. It is a panorama of images from all nature & art, whereon the sun & stars shine but go up to it & nothing is there.   (JMN, V, 255)

The central images of Emerson's essays shimmer partly because he believed that Reason glimpsed the spiritual truths they embody only momentarily and partly because their meaning cannot be fully fathomed. "The aim of the author is not to tell truth—that he cannot do, but to suggest it," Emerson noted in 1835; "he has only approximated it himself, & hence . . . he uses many words, hoping that one, if not another, will bring you as near to the fact as he is" (JMN, V, 51). On another occasion Emerson wrote: "As the musician avails himself of the concert, so the philosopher avails himself of the drama, the epic, the novel, & becomes a poet; for these complex forms allow of the utterance of his knowledge of life by *indirections* as well in the didactic way, & can therefore express the fluxional quantities & values which the thesis or dissertation could never give" (JMN, VII, 190).

Flashing momentarily on the inner eye, an Emersonian hieroglyph is to be intuited; its final impression is not to be so much any concrete thought communicated by sentences as it is to be the effect of the whole stimulating instinct (which initiates the sequence leading to new plateaus of thought). Thus hieroglyphs function like those of Egyptian priests, not because symbols need to be protected from vulgar minds but because in its present state the human mind is vulgar. In accord with Platonic pedagogy, albeit for somewhat different reasons, Emerson combines a didactic with a secretive manner. Warner Berthoff is quite correct in pointing out Emerson's "laconic fitness of thought and phrase which can release yet at the same time perfectly conceal some momentous stroke of understanding." [28] One can account for this effect by acknowledging that Emerson's notions pertaining to hieroglyphics are a fundamental feature of his artistic practice.

The central hieroglyph or image unifies an essay, allowing Emerson to discard the general step-by-step, logical mode of expression. Each essay was to be "miscellaneous" in its shape, its author "adding and adding, instead of developing."

This idea did not free Emerson from acute sensitivity to each word—"its place in the sentence should make its emphasis" (JMN, IV, 273)—nor relieve him from obligations regarding sentences. Indeed, approaching an essay as if it were a painting demanded precision in use of words and sentences, because both are equivalent to brush strokes—not overly interesting in themselves but invaluable in a cumulative effect. The sentence is important but is not, as F.O. Matthiessen and others have argued, Emerson's artistic unit. [29]

Emerson's view of the sentence is perhaps best expressed in a journal entry for 1845: "I think the Platonists may be read for sentences, though the reader fail to grasp the argument of the paragraph or the chapter. He may yet obtain gleams & glimpses of a more excellent illumination from their genius outvaluing the most distinct information he owes to other books. The grandeur of the impression the stars & heavenly bodies make on us is surely more valuable than our exact perception of a tub or a table on the ground" (JMN, IX, 261). These sentences succeed not as unique units but as conveyers of "gleams & glimpses," as impressions of the larger whole in which they participate. Emerson also is a master of the epigrammatic sentence and of the provocative proverb, but these devices only entice the reader's mind to penetrate beyond its superficial level of perception and to glimpse the larger whole, the more hidden mystery, in the revelation of which these devices play a minor but contributory part.

For Emerson, sentences are inadequate units of organization. In a notebook entry he explained that, whereas one stanza of a poem is complete, "one sentence of prose is not" (JMN, VII, 316). Arrangement and order loomed large in Emerson's mind: "Profoundest thoughts, sublime images, dazzling figures are squandered & lost in an immethodical harangue" (JMN, V, 409). Emerson's writings are replete with references to the architectural design of genuine art, as, for example, when he speaks of "that species of architecture which I study & practice, namely, Rhetoric or the Building of Discourse" (JMN, V, 409). "Great design belongs to a poem," he later wrote; "we want an architect" (W, VIII, 33). As in a painting, such a design engenders an overall impression. The artist is to use the "tool of Synthesis" in combining "every link in [the] living chain he found separate" so that "the composition has manifold the effect of the component parts" (JMN, V, 39). The important word in this comment is *effect*. Every sentence, every stroke of the artist's brush, may be as brilliant as a gem; but the heightened *effect* of each precious stone depends finally on its setting.

In "The Naturalist" and later in a lecture on Shakespeare

(1835) and in a poem entitled "Each and All" (1839), Emerson clearly indicates his belief in the artistic conjunction of design and effect: "Composition is more important than the elegance of individual forms. Every artist knows that beyond its own beauty the object has an additional grace from relation to surrounding objects. The most elegant shell in your cabinet does not produce such *effect* on the eye *as the contrast and combination of a group of ordinary sea shells lying together wet upon the beach*" (EL, I, 73; italics added). A word, a sentence, a proverb may indeed be elegant, but each becomes even more resplendent in an apt setting. The difference lies in Emerson's distinction between mere detail and artistic effect. The specific words, the individual sentence units in Emerson's best essays, perform like "ordinary sea shells lying together wet upon the beach"; their miscellaneous beauty becomes a hieroglyph imparting a collective visual impression or effect to the reader's inner eye.

This effect is fleeting for reasons already mentioned. Similarly the artist's design producing this effect should also disappear. Like the literati of the Egyptian hieroglyphics, though for different reasons noted, Emerson maintained that "the wary artist . . . will tear down the scaffolding when the Work is finished & himself supply no clew to the curiosity that would know how he did the wonder" (JMN, IV, 363). This notion informs Emerson's complaint that Hawthorne "invites his readers too much into his study, opens the process before them. As if the confectioner should say to his customers Now let us make the cake" (JMN, IX, 405).[30] The beauty of Emerson's prose poems or prose paintings, in contrast, remains simultaneously miscellaneous yet designed. The individual sentences mimetically convey the swirl or flux of life, whereas the dimly perceived yet central and organizing hieroglyph to which they aesthetically contribute represents the spiritual unity beneath all particulars. One might venture the conclusion, from another angle of vision, that Emerson's antinomian stress on feeling always was balanced, in his artistry as well as in his thought, by a unitarian emphasis on order.

To provide a visual aesthetic effect, to color the line of his thought as expressed in sentences, Emerson made substantial use of image clusters and motifs which "picture forth" the central hieroglyph. Throughout the essays reviewed in the following chapters, imagery participates in units or chains, which in turn participate in a governing hieroglyph; none are independent. Links between the various clusters are not always logical. After "The America Scholar" (1837) images or clusters do not necessarily partake of some sequential pattern. They obey the laws of the Imagination rather than those of the Fancy: "The Fancy takes the world as it stands & selects pleasing groups by apparent relations. The Imagination is Vision, regards the world as symbolical & pierces the emblem for the real sense, sees all external objects as types" (JMN, V, 76).

Like the Neoplatonists he read, Emerson relied on an intuitive sense of how one image engenders another. Consequently, although transitions between these images always exist, they may derive from some similar function, some kinship in configuration, or some more abstruse relationship perceived in their mutual intrinsic meaning. Whenever Emerson coalesces imagery, he does so in response to an intuitive, poetic sense of the correspondence of one with the other—the exact talent he most admired in George Herbert.

This procedure might have proved a formidable obstacle to the literary critic had not Emerson been somewhat restricted in the range of his imagery. Most frequently image patterns in a particular essay derive from a hieroglyph and its related motifs in another essay. In one sense Emerson was indeed making "the same objects exponents of his new thought." Just as "every word has a double, treble or centuple use and meaning" (W, VI, 304), so too do the natural images mirrored in words: "In nature, each individual symbol plays innumerable parts, as each particle of matter circulates in turn through every system" (W, IV, 121). Emerson readily expanded one system of imagery into another with a resultant coalescing dictated less by arbitrary whim than by what he believed to be his intuitive discernment of the inherent sign-value and relationships shared.

By making these images the exponents of his new thought, Emerson became a poet as he defined the role, penetrating the successive layers of spiritual significance pictured in the hieroglyphics of nature. This ability is what he admired most not only in the so-called metaphysical poets of the seventeenth century but in Plato as well, who elevated "every fact to successive platforms and so disclos[ed] in every fact a germ of expansion" (W, IV, 81).

Imagery, seemingly miscellaneous but finally as integrated in a central hieroglyph as are the vehicular sentences, is the essence of Emerson's prose artistry. His prose is poetic prose. Although his poems generally may prove less appealing than his prose, it should be noted that Emerson himself was very dubious about his poems and tended to think of his vocation as that of a prose poet (L, I, 435).[31]

It is true that in 1822, when he did not yet possess the artistic sensibility he developed later, he indicated that "the language of the passions . . . do not ordinarily find their full expression in the sober strain of prose" (JMN, I, 63; also, V, 51). But even this statement, which he later crossed out, is qualified by the word *ordinarily*.

At the end of his career he would know and proudly declare that "there are also prose poets," that next to poetry there is "poetic prose" (W, VIII, 50; JMN, IX, 172). Through the medium of *poetic* prose, through organization of an essay around a central hieroglyph and coalescing imagery in relation to this governing image, Emerson successfully surmounted what he considered the chief limitation of prose: "that we cannot strongly state one fact without seeming to belie some other" (W, II, 39). Only through the centrally organizing picture of a hieroglyph could Emerson present several facts simultaneously and convey a fleeting intuitive glimpse of their underlying unity.

Part 2: *Practice*

II

The One Man Hieroglyph

In "The American Scholar"

Our discussion of Emerson's literary practice begins with "The American Scholar" (1837) because that essay marks an important stage in the development of its author's thought and artistry.

Discussions of this essay generally have concentrated on its relation to Emerson's life and ideas,[1] but a notable exception is Richard P. Adams' excellent investigation of Emerson's use of the organic metaphor, specifically the formula derived from the living plant.[2] Adams' article provides a stepping-stone to closer examination of Emerson's literary technique in "The American Scholar," a careful reading of which indicates that, although vestiges of more formal features of discursive writing are present—as we remarked in Chapter 1, order and method were very much on Emerson's mind in 1837 (JMN, V, 409)— the essay also possesses several related, consciously fashioned images which collectively serve as a structuring motif. This imagery, particularly as it finally relates to the notion of the One Man, represents Emerson's experiment with a mode of internal organization which in later essays totally supplants the artificial external method of arrangement evident, for instance, in the formal divisions of "The American Scholar." In this early essay the experiment is only partially successful, for the inner structure of image clusters relating to nature as well as to man's body and mind threatens to become as rigid and static as the external method it is designed to replace. Although the idea of the One

Man unites these images, the essay does not quite achieve the sort of governing central hieroglyph present in many later writings; in this regard, it may be pertinent to recall that Emerson recommended the review on Chinese characters and Egyptian hieroglyphics to Margaret Fuller fourteen months after his delivery of "The American Scholar" as an address at Cambridge.

Emerson perfected his use of a hieroglyph as an aesthetic device, as the ordering visual center of an essay, during 1837 and 1838. Nevertheless, motifs of "The American Scholar"— which provide something of a coda for the prominent imagery in later essays—are meant to contribute collectively to a visual impression of the scholar as a person who realizes "the philosophy of the erect position" by abandoning his previous divided condition, rising to his feet, and approaching spiritual wholeness (JMN, IV, 333; cf. Milton, a major influence on Emerson, in *Paradise Lost*, VII, 507–10).

The first formal division of "The American Scholar" considers the influence of nature on the scholar. Here Emerson introduces a tripartite sequence of images, in ascending order, based on root, stem, and flower. He instructs us to discover "roots running under ground, whereby contrary and remote things cohere, and flower out from one stem" and to realize that nature and man "proceed from one root; one is leaf and one is flower" (CW, I, 54, 55). For Emerson, the most beautiful part of the plant appropriately appears in the upper regions, which in essay after essay symbolize the spiritual realm. In part this beauty includes the fact that from flowers come fruits. Throughout "The American Scholar" *fruit* operates as a metaphor for what mankind someday may achieve, and it is disgraceful "not to yield that peculiar fruit which each man was created to bear" (CW, I, 69). The ideal scholar, whose every deed detaches "itself from the life like a ripe fruit," will become "the apple which the ages have desired to pluck, now at last ripe, and inviting nations to the harvest"; others will see in him "their own green and crude being,—ripened" (CW, I, 60, 64, 65).

Whereas the image cluster of root, stem, flower, and fruit is well developed, the complementary sequence of earth, air, and sky is barely suggested (it is to be used more extensively in later essays). This excerpt presents the series: "Every day, the sun; and, after sunset, night and her stars. Ever the winds blow; ever the grass grows" (CW, I, 54). The preceding sequence shows how Emerson tries to suggest motion within the categories, thereby preventing them from being mere static coordinates. The sky, like the flower, crowns this sequence; significantly the stars, a synecdoche for the sky, appear later when Emerson explains that the scholar sits "in his private observatory, cataloguing obscure and nebulous stars of the human mind" (CW, I, 62). This astronomy of thought is a correlative for the fruit the scholar bears, an idea equally evident in the image of an aster in Emerson's poem, "The Apology" (1846).

Both image clusters—root-stem-flower and earth-air-sky—finally relate to man, specifically to a third image sequence pertaining to the human body: "We no more feel or know [our present act], than we feel the feet, or the hand, or the brain of our body" (CW, I, 60). Man's feet, hands, and head represent parallel correlatives to nature's root (earth), stem (air), and flower (sky). That Emerson equates the human head to the sky is evident in his reference to the scholar's effort to chart an astronomy of the mind; that he associates it with the flower is clear in an instance of humor, subtly derived from his motif, when he remarks about the impropriety of the person who hides "his head like an ostrich in the flowering bushes" (CW, I, 64). Significantly this comment is a conflation of two journal entries (JMN, V, 248, 330), which only in their final version emphasize Emerson's point about the human head; for in his scheme heads, like flowers and stars, are by their nature designed for ascent. Ironically, in spite of nature's floral reminder of his proper position, the person perversely hiding his head absurdly thrusts upward an inappropriate portion of his anatomy.[3]

Throughout his essay Emerson transforms the basic order

of the feet-hands-head sequence into a more complex amalga-
mation of images. He expands references to extremities of the
body to include the actions of walking, working, and thinking.
Concerning his feet, the scholar avoids "treading the old road"
because he seeks to awaken men from their "sleep-walking"
(CW, I, 101, 65).⁴ He especially walks or travels within his
own mind: "Success treads on every right step. For the instinct
is sure that prompts him to tell his brother what he thinks. He
then learns that in going down into the secrets of his own
mind, he has descended into the secrets of all minds" (CW, I,
63). That Emerson relates feet and instinct in this passage is
an important point.

Emerson makes even greater use of hand imagery. The
word *hand,* occurring many times in this and other writings, is
most often associated with labor. Since our recent actions comprise "the business which we now have in hand," it is impera-
tive to realize the truth of the proverb that "all things have
two handles. Beware of the wrong one" (CW, I, 60, 54). The
scholar, therefore, must not merely follow the instincts of his
feet; he must also will or act with his hands. Contrary to popular belief, Emerson explains in imagery relating to manual toil,
the scholar is not "as unfit for any handiwork or public labor,
as a penknife for an axe"; rather his deeds actually give expression to the divine nature within mankind, for "as the world
was plastic and fluid in the hands of God, so it is ever to so
much of his attributes as we bring to it" (CW, I, 59, 64). The
principal benefit from the work of the scholar's hands, his
divine handiwork, is the steady movement of mankind toward
unity and brotherhood. Thus, speaking in the persona of the
scholar, Emerson says: "I grasp the hands of those next [to]
me, and take my place in the ring to suffer and to work" (CW,
I, 59).

The corespondence between nature imagery and that of the
human body is even more pronounced in references to the
employment of hands in the activity of farming. Frequently
he stresses the manual tools used in farming: "There is virtue

yet in the hoe and the spade, for learned as well as for un-
learned hands" (CW, I, 62). Farming serves as a metaphor
yoking man and nature in a relationship implying action, in
contrast to the stasis his categories might otherwise suggest,
and implying a union in which the two component parts cannot be meaningfully distinguished. The final emphasis of "The
American Scholar" falls upon the purpose of farming, namely
the ripening of fruits and the gathering of harvests. Later, in
"Prudence," Emerson treats the farm as a central hieroglyph.

As one might predict from the other sequences, the head
is the crowning feature of the three extremities of the body,
and so the scholar aptly sits at "the head of the table" (CW, I,
64). Just as the flower depends on the stem and leaves, the
scholar's head requires the body's hands and actions. Without
action, without the photosynthesizing leaves of the body,
"thought can never ripen into truth"; for "he who has put forth
his total strength in fit actions, has the richest return of wisdom" (CW, I, 59, 60). Nevertheless, the stem is hierarchically
lower than the flower and action remains subordinate to
thought (CW, I, 59).[5]

Emerson fashions still another parallel image cluster to
characterize thought. In the opening paragraph of the essay
he refers to the "ancient Greeks," the "Troubadours," and "our
contemporaries," allusions which become clearer later in the
work: "Historically, there is thought to be a difference in the
ideas which predominate over successive epochs, and there are
data for marking the genius of the Classic, of the Romantic,
and now of the Reflective or Philosophical age" (CW, I, 66).
To this remark Emerson adds: "each individual passes through
all three. The boy is a Greek; the youth, romantic; the adult,
reflective."[6] An upward progression, corresponding to that of
the other sequences, is quite apparent in his differentiation of
these historical and ontogenic phases.

Emerson approaches intellection in terms of still another
tripartite series: seeing, thinking, and speaking. This sequence,

the sixth in the essay, discloses more explicitly what Emerson means by the thinking stage of the walking-working-thinking image cluster. The three components of the former series have been rightly the subject of much critical attention,[7] so few basic facets of its presence as a motif need to be noted. In contrast to the average man's "sluggard intellect" peering "from under its iron lids," the scholar "speculates" (CW, I, 52, 59). As the Latin meaning of *specula* (watchtower) intimates, the scholar possesses distant vision, sees widely from the lofty elevation of his foresight. The importance of vision, distant as opposed to near, is crucial to Emerson's beliefs and particularly relevant to his aesthetic based on the visual whole of the "distant" hieroglyph, not on the particulars of "near" sentences. What the scholar sees, however, must be transformed through the mysterious process which is not labeled in the essay but which is the will, the inexplicable principle of animation resulting in thought. This process comprises mental work or action and is intimated evasively: "The preamble of thought, the transition through which it passes from the unconscious to the conscious, is action" (CW, I, 59). In this sequence of upward progression, the unconscious is equivalent to seeing, to instinct, to the feet ("we see with our feet," CW, I, 66); the act of transition is the very dynamics or animation of the thought process, which begins with seeing and is related to the will, to the hands; consciousness, the flower of thought and the fruit of truth, corresponds to speaking, to the head.[8] As man thinking, that is to say as one who genuinely participates in all three phases of intellection (perceiving, speaking, and the elusive dynamic uniting them into a process), the scholar "sees absolute truth; and utters truth, or creates" (CW, I, 56).

Emerson expresses this sequence in still another manner: "experience is converted into thought, as a mulberry leaf is converted into satin" (CW, I, 59). Leaflike action or experience is internally and mysteriously transformed into conscious thought.

The following diagram may make these relationships clearer:

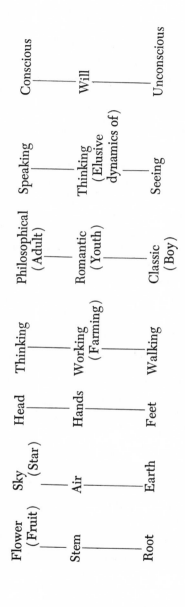

This diagram shows not only the parallel aspects of Emerson's sequences but also how they steadily move toward defining the internal nature of the human mind. He uses these related series to eradicate any sense of separation between the exterior world of nature and the interior realm of the mind. Thus, "the deeper [the scholar] dives into his privatest secretest presentiment,—to his wonder he finds, this is the most acceptable, most public, and universally true" (CW, I, 63). In "Wealth" (1860), which like many other writings develops imagery in "The American Scholar," Emerson explains precisely what he has tried to depict in the earlier essay. In the later work he asserts that nothing exists in the world which is not duplicated in man's body, "a sort of miniature or summary of the world." He adds: "there is nothing in his body which is not repeated as in a celestial sphere in his mind . . . there is nothing in his brain which is not repeated in a higher sphere in his moral system" (W, VI, 124–25).

The notion that what is private really is public, that what is external in nature and history actually is internal in the self accounts for images of circularity in "The American Scholar": "there is never a beginning, there is never an end to the inexplicable continuity of this web of God, but always circular power returning into itself"; "the stream retreats to its source" (CW, I, 54, 61). Such imagery reinforces the emphasis of other motifs on the correspondence between nature and the human mind.

At first, the very hierarchical scheme informing the imagistic framework of "The American Scholar" seems antithetical to this stress on circularity. But verticality, a progressive verticality or spiral, is a key Emersonian image for the process of inward expansion. Vertical categories in "The American Scholar" merely represent an early expression of this spiral which Emerson dramatized more successfully later.

Apparently aware of the problem of overschematization posed by his variety of sequences, Emerson tried to avoid a simple and merely linear diagrammatic framework. "I do not much dwell on these differences," he says of one sequence

(CW, I, 66). In rejecting the formal logic and techniques of the eighteenth century, Emerson wanted to curtail such schematization.[9] Although he never dismissed these vertical hierarchies—a symbolic system was a prerequisite for knowledge—he managed them somewhat less stiffly in later writings.

Even in "The American Scholar" he aimed for a sense of dynamics in the scheme. One of his solutions lies within the diagram itself and implicitly relates to the image of circularity that at first seems contrary to the sequences. In the feet-hands-head series the direction of the process is from the bottom toward the top; the process is also one of external stimulus steadily internalized. In the series comprised of seeing, the dynamics of thinking, and speaking the process is paradoxically reversed in spite of the fact that the parts of the sequence are directly equivalent to those of the feet-hands-head series. In the process of intellection the direction is from the upper region of the head (eyes) downward toward the lower region (mouth); the process is also one of an internalized stimulus externalized in speech. This paradox suggests a core as elusive as the second facet of the intellection process, a mystical center beyond vision and articulation of any sort which is the very animating principle of the entire system. This center lies within "the inexplicable continuity of this web of God."

Emerson uses another related technique to impart a sense of circular dynamic to his scheme, as well as to stress the correspondence between man and nature. Often he complexly interweaves images, substituting one image for its parallel in another sequence. Consider the following example:

> It is a great stride. It is a sign—is it not? of new vigor, when the extremities are made active, when currents of warm life run into the hands and the feet. I ask not for the great, the remote, the romantic; what is doing in Italy or Arabia; what is Greek art, or Provençal Minstrelsy; I embrace the common, I explore and sit at the feet of the familiar, the low. Give me insight into to-day, and you may have the antique and future worlds. What would we really know the meaning of? . . . the glance of the eye; the form and the gait of the body;—show me the ultimate reason of these matters;—show me the sublime

presence of the highest spiritual cause lurking, as always it does
lurk, in these suburbs and extremities of nature.

(CW, I, 67–68)

The intermingling of correspondent images from various sequences makes clear, among other matters, that the separation
between nature and man intrinsic to schematization is an illusion. The very designation of the extremities implied by the
imagery—though not of its inner principle of ascent—is something of a deception. As Emerson explicitly insists and as his
interwoven imagery and paradoxical circularity of sequences
implicitly demonstrate, the fact is that "the near explains the
far" because "one design unites and animates the farthest pinnacle and the lowest trench" (CW, I, 68). Similarly, when one
truly possesses an active soul, then he becomes a whole man
not separable into such parts as head, hands, and feet. Only in
"the *divided* or social state" people "have suffered amputation
from the trunk, and strut about so many walking monsters,—a
good finger, a neck, a stomach, an elbow, but never a man"
(CW, I, 53).

Emerson sought to counter man's truncated perception of
life's extremities by using them as a structuring device. As the
preceding discussion of his aesthetic theory suggests and as
analyses to follow clarify, these images were not meant to attract attention to themselves individually or even as clusters.
They were to remain semivisible within the swirl of prose
(another technique for conveying a sense of motion to sequences); they were to impart subtly and unobtrusively to the
intuitive eye of Reason a diffused sensation of the ultimate
unity permeating the numerous particulars of creation.

In short, the audience must participate with the artist in
still another facet of the paradoxical circularity of these vertical
sequences; for "one nature wrote and the same reads" with the
result that "there is . . . creative reading, as well as creative
writing" (CW, I, 57, 58). This circular bond between artist
and audience occurs because the conscious thought the artist
utters, the transformation of his unconscious instinct through
his will, stimulates the instinct of his reader or hearer, thereby

initiating in his audience that impulse which will generate still another thought. In "The American Scholar," the cumulative effect of Emerson's artistry, operating at a nearly subliminal level, communicates a visual impression of how mankind's approach to unity, as exemplified in the scholar, is based on nature's inner principle of ascent.

Emerson's covert focus in the essay on the number *three* is significant in this context. Not only does each image sequence separate into three parts but the essay also is divided formally into three sections. Particularly noteworthy is the relation of this number to the fable of the One Man introducing the essay. Although critics have identified Emerson's sources for this fable as Plato, Plutarch, and Empedocles of Acrogas,[10] they have not discussed the function of the number *three* in the essay. Traditionally this number signifies unity or spiritual synthesis; Emerson surely was aware of its meaning with regard to the Christian trinity and to the Pythagorean doctrine of secret numbers.[11] In "The American Scholar" the number *three*, an adjunct to the central image of the One Man, serves as something of a secret formula for the spiritual reunification of mankind.

Through the modulated control of the structuring motifs in "The American Scholar" Emerson sought to bypass that part of his reader which does not perceive "how a globule of sap ascends" and to appeal directly to the inner eye which intuitively "aspire[s] to the highest" (CW, I, 69, 65). Appropriately, then, Emerson concludes the essay with a portrait of a man who, no longer divided into parts or unnaturally hiding his head in flowering bushes, is coming together, rising, and standing on his own feet. After noting that "young men . . . do not yet see [use the feet of the intellect], that if the single man plant [use his hands in metaphoric farming] himself indomitably on his instincts [use his feet], and there abide, the huge world will come round to him [reveal its circularity]," he concludes: "we will walk on our own feet; we will work with our own hands; we will speak our own minds" (CW, I, 69–70). In this image of the scholar as a whole man, Emerson presents a microcosmic representation of the macrocosmic One Man. More significantly, this image of the scholar serves as the central picture toward which all image clusters point; in this sense it functions very similarly to Emerson's later, more accomplished use of a hieroglyph as the governing center of an essay.

Although later Emerson successfully experimented with this technique and specifically modified or expanded certain images in "The American Scholar," the basic hierarchical associations established in it provide foundation for the imagery of subsequent writings. Even in such a late work as *English Traits* (1856), which represents no artistic achievement in terms of the aesthetic I am trying to define, images derived from the hieroglyph of the One Man furnish a certain, though loose, structural underpinning.[12]

In "Politics"

"Politics" (1844) provides an interesting example of how Emerson worked within the context of the One Man image without repeating himself. Replete with references to necessity, it is more darkly toned than "The American Scholar"; but its development of the One Man hieroglyph attests to an optimism akin to, even if less intense than, that of the earlier essay.

The meaning of the word *politics* (of a citizen) no doubt suggested the propriety of using the hieroglyph of the One Man. For Emerson, the state is a composite of all men and does not represent them merely in the sense of delegated authority but also in the sense that it portrays or manifests all men in large. In a sentence not in the lecture version of the present essay passage (EL, III, 241)—hence suggesting its importance to the scheme of the published version—Emerson combines this idea about the state and the economic metaphor running throughout when he explains that American laws are "a currency which we stamp with our own portrait" (W, III, 200). The darker cast of his thinking leads Emerson to stress the infantile stage of the One Man reflected on this legal coinage or laws.

This stage is represented, in the double sense of something delegated to a proxy and of something depicted on a coin, by America's political parties, which appear divided into opposite sides. Emerson conceded that in life there is a ground of necessity particularly evident in polarity; indeed "the fact of two poles, of two forces, centripetal and centrifugal, is universal" (W, III, 212). American political systems mirror this universal fact, especially with regard to the tension between persons and property, "the two objects for whose protection government exists" (W, III, 201). Whereas the conservatively timid Whigs are "defensive of property," the radical, aimless Democrats prove selfishly destructive (W, III, 210).[13] In Emerson's opinion, both polar extremes have their own subsequent "weight," which keeps earthbound the political system and the One Man *represented* by that system.

Unable to stand erect, this earthbound One Man seems more an infant than an adult. The timid defensiveness of the Whigs and the aimless selfishness of the Democrats merely reflect childishness.[14] In this infantile stage, we lack "the tranquillity of the strong when we walk abroad" and so we must "climb" and "crawl" (W, III, 218). Only when "the public mind is opened to more intelligence," only when the One Man begins to mature, will our legal coinage in restrospect "seem to be brute and stammering" (W, III, 201). Because at present this legal coinage *represents* human childishness, "it speaks not articulately" (W, III, 201).

The impulse toward maturity provides the vertical force countering the weight or horizontal thrust of necessity—a variation of a motif recurrent throughout *Essays: Second Series*. With maturity the One Man will stand erect and thereby fulfill the destiny of men and of their collective image reflected in politics, a destiny which Emerson believes is self-evident in the underlying meaning of the words that people (and the essay under discussion) use over and over again with regard to government. Such words as *state, statute,* and *institution* all derive from the root *sta* meaning *to stand.* To stand is man's destiny. Emerson notes that the student of politics actually studies man's slow but steady development from crawling and climbing toward balanced standing. "The history of the State," or the account of the One Man rising, "sketches in coarse outline the progress of thought" (W, III, 201) because, as the human intellect matures, the One Man gains perspective on his former infantile statutes, on that legal coinage bearing his image, and eventually *rises* above them.

Thus the state reflects the inner spirit of the One Man, which spirit, as "The American Scholar" indicated, aspires to the highest. In "Politics" Emerson makes clear that human "aspiration" is what the history of the state "follows at a distance" (W, III, 201). This principle of vertical ascent is evident in the unuttered dreams of poetic youths, in intuitions which "shall presently be the resolutions of public bodies" (W, III, 201). Insensitivity to this principle accounts for the mistaken impression that society lies "in rigid repose" (W, III, 199)—the emphatic *rigid* did not appear in the lecture version (EL, III, 240)—that society is dead and not merely asleep, that its horizontal features preclude vertical possibilities. The poetic youth senses and the wise man knows, however, that even the horizontal field of necessity is fluid rather than rigid, that (in Hegelian manner) each polar "force by its own activity develops the other" (W, III, 212). Consequently the restraint of law balances the desire for liberty and vice versa. Because the horizontal weight of necessity in reality is fluid and not impenetrably rigid, the principle of vertical human aspiration operates in a plastic matrix through which it can ascend. Vertical ascent, in the individual and in the One Man represented by the state, manifests maturation. This growth has no limit: "the boundaries of personal influence" prove "impossible to fix" (W, III, 205). Man aspires to the highest— Emerson deliberately avoids trying to define specifically what constitutes the highest because he regards the process of ascent as eternal and its goal forever elusive. This feature of thought

and artistic practice becomes even more apparent in other essays; but now let us focus on Emerson's conclusion in "Politics"
that, in spite of the *weight* of necessity, man and the state
mature in direct proportion to the ascent of ideas.

To develop this idea of ascent, Emerson selected the image
of a building or house under construction as another facet of
the One Man hieroglyph. This is not a new device, as subsequent discussions of earlier essays will demonstrate. Its appropriateness does not derive from any logical relation between a
house and a man; their affinity arises from an inherent pictorial
correspondence or configuration. The sort of analogy implied
by Emerson recalls that used by several of his favorite seventeenth-century English poets. In fact, the primary source for
this house feature of the hieroglyph in "Politics" may well be
George Herbert's "Man," a poem which speaks of man as a
house and which Emerson quotes in *Nature*, in "Demonology,"
and frequently in his journals (CW, I, 40–41; EL, III, 158;
JMN, III, 255; VI, 103; IX, 278). For Emerson, the state is a
building, an institution of defense; the state is designed for
protection of people and property. If citizens who comprise
the One Man fail to "build on Ideas" (W, III, 200), if they
fail to continue to construct toward the highest after each preceding level has been attained, they then do more damage than
good by using their fortress-like building-of-state perversely to
guard against maturity (standing). The genuine citizen, however, will be wary of every "blunder which *stands* in colossal
ugliness in the governments of the world," of every "*structure*"
which permits "the rich to *encroach* on the poor," of every
political party which quits the "natural *ground*" for the "*defence* of points nowise belonging to their system" (W, III, 214,
204, 208; italics added).

As thought and the One Man mature, this building of defense, which is the state, will ascend. Then the "watch-towers"
will be manned "by better guards" (W, III, 202, 204); then
political parties will survey "the deep and necessary grounds to
which they are respectively entitled" (W, III, 209). Progres-
sively "the broad design of renovating the State on the prin-

ciple of right and love" will be realized (W, III, 221). Such construction or maturation depends, Emerson puns in the final paragraph, on recognition that "we live in a very low state" (W, III, 220). In his opinion the building-of-state fails to defend its citizens when it has not been constructed sufficiently high on successive "necessary grounds" or foundations, when it reflects the "low state," the crawling and climbing of the immature One Man whom the state represents, in two senses of the word. A new foundation and a further elevation of the state and its citizens (the One Man) would lead to repudiation of the current selfish and childish ground of America's political parties and subsequently to "recognition of *higher* rights than those of personal freedom [Democrats], or the security of property [Whigs]" (W, III, 219; italics added). Transformation would be allowed from the low state of "parties of circumstance" whose members ironically "stand for the defence of those interests in which they find themselves" (W, III, 208–209) into the higher state of parties of principle.

Again, using techniques similar to those in the seventeenth-century poetry he read, Emerson "builds into" his essay another motif, dependent on the word *principle*, bearing directly on the image of man's ascent but significantly at a higher, more abstract level of the reader's intellectual perception. When man matures, when the state which is himself is constructed upwardly on successive *principles* that provide an ever-new foundation, then the *princely* feature of humanity is made manifest. True ascent is not only a maturation and a construction but also the "coronation of [nature's] king" (W, III, 216).

When each citizen participates in this princely One Man, whose "grandeur of character" (W, III, 217) is upwardly aspiring principle informing the construction of the state—note in the following passage a specifically American metaphor alluding to the Revolutionary War—we will no longer "pay unwilling tribute" (W, III, 220);[15] then the state, its statutes (that "currency which we stamp with our own portrait"), and its citizens will all be one and the same. Ideally the ultimate royal principle of love will. form the true foundation; then the state will be "a knot of friends" rather than "a rope of sand which perishes in the twisting" (W, III, 221, 200).

The final focus of "Politics" falls on this princely potentiality of the maturing One Man (the macrocosmic citizen, the controlling visual image at the core of the essay) and on his alter ego, the emerging protective building-of-state—that is, on the human potentiality to stand upright pictorially implicit in the word *state*.

In "Spiritual Laws"

Between the presentation of "The American Scholar" and the publication of "Politics," Emerson used the One Man hieroglyph somewhat differently in "Spiritual Laws" (1841). Apparently discontent over too-evident specificity of categories in "The American Scholar," Emerson seems deliberately to have made the central image of the One Man vaguer. He wanted to achieve a subtler management of the hieroglyph to actualize better its subliminal function. Particularly pertinent to this subliminal feature of his aesthetics is Emerson's notion that people reason "from the seen to the unseen"; the muted hieroglyph of the One Man in "Spiritual Laws" is designed to frustrate the "superstitions of sense," the "trick of the senses" (W, II, 146, 161, 163). In other words, were the underlying governing image of the essay to emerge too concretely or specifically, it would reinforce man's sensuous dependence on natural phenomena as ultimate reality. Consequently Emerson dissolves the external anthropomorphic features of the One Man and bases his hieroglyph on the circulatory system, on an internal and hidden aspect of man.

In this way Emerson puts his basic image to good use yet manages to convey more easily that sense of progression which *seemed* at variance with the tripartite categories in "The American Scholar." He succeeds in imparting to the reader's inner eye an impression, a mental sensation in contrast to one derived from highly specified imagery, of some ultimate organic wholeness underlying and informing the apparent chaos of surface particulars. In "Spiritual Laws" the reader feels as if he were on the threshold of seeing this ultimate organic something, but it always eludes his focusing capacity. This blurry image is intentional; subliminally sensed, it remains too "distant" for the reader's "near" vision to clarify. As a result the reader actually participates in an experience of the fact, as Emerson presents it, that mankind engages in partial acts, "the choice of the hands, of the eyes, of the appetites, and not a whole act of the man" (W, II, 140). Moreover, men cannot contemplate the One Man because they are part of him, a mere organ—"all things are its organs" (W, II, 155; cf. 163). A part cannot know the whole, an internal organ cannot discern the external features of that of which it is a part. "Spiritual Laws" represents a brilliant illustration of the harmonious interaction of Emerson's thought and aesthetics.

Before saying more about the image of circulation in the essay, it is necessary to discuss a reinforcing motif pertaining to the Biblical myth of the Fall and to indicate how this motif functions in terms of Emerson's notion of the transforming power designated as the will. In Christian tradition—and "Spiritual Laws" is replete not only with usages drawn from this tradition but with Biblical allusions [16]—the will is man's central faculty in pre- and postlapsarian times. The will is responsible for sin and ultimately it provides the chief locus for the conversion experience. Emerson echoes many of these conventional ideas in "Spiritual Laws," and in particular repudiates the common belief that certain people are great because of the unique capacity of their individual wills. On the contrary, he argues in alliance with general Christian notions of saintliness, "that which externally seemed will and immovableness was willingness and self-annihilation" (W, II, 134).

If Emerson agrees with Christian tradition about the nature of the regenerate will, he disagrees concerning its view of the myth of the Fall. For him the Fall represents a *felix culpa* (a fortunate fall), its legend merely an allegory of how the will and nature normally and healthfully operate. To approach the myth of the Fall from the traditional point of view is to be "diseased with the theological problems of original sin" (W, II, 132).

It is a fact of life, he explains, that everything participates in the action of falling, a lesson readily taught by the Book of Nature (the book image belongs to still another motif in the essay and derives from the medieval notion, still popular in the seventeenth century, of the two great Books of Scripture and Nature):

> Let us draw a lesson from nature, which always works by short ways. When the fruit is ripe, it falls. When the fruit is despatched, the leaf falls. The circuit of the waters is mere falling. The walking of man and all animals is a falling forward. All our manual labor and works of strength, as prying, splitting, digging, rowing and so forth, are done by dint of continual falling, and the globe, earth, moon, comet, sun, star, fall for ever and ever.   (W, II, 137)

In accord with the design of nature all forms eventually fall away. Such centers of momentary attraction as great men and great books must fall away in order that new forms may arise. By this process "the great soul" enshrines "itself in some other form" and performs "some other deed"; these in turn become the new "flower and head of all living nature" (W, II, 166)— imagery recalling hierarchical schemes in "The American Scholar."

For Emerson, then, the meaning of the Biblical myth of the Fall is true but not as interpreted by Christian fundamentalists. Man, like everything else in creation, falls so that he may improve. Through exercise of the will in the instance of Adam's Fall and subsequently in that of our own actions, mankind increasingly develops consciousness (note in the excerpt "Let us draw a lesson from nature . . ." just cited that the will once again is depicted through images of work). Such falls consequently always prove fortunate in the fullest optimistic sense for Emerson, who even later in his life never shared Nathaniel Hawthorne's darker version of this notion of *felix culpa*. Like the authors of seventeenth-century religious poetry, Emerson stresses the Christian notion that every spiritual fall is followed by a joyful reemergence, that death yields to everlasting life. This seemingly paradoxical interrelatedness of falling and rising, of the horizontal and the vertical, pertains directly to Emerson's epigrammatic remark that "the height of the pinnacle is determined by the breadth of the base" (W, II, 141).

This process of falling and rising manifests the principle of universal circulation in the One Man, the principle to which Emerson alludes by metonymy when he speaks of "the circuit of the waters" as a "mere falling" (again see excerpt "Let us draw a lesson from nature . . ." just cited). In making this point, he counters traditional Christian interpretation of the Fall, an assault on conventions reinforced by the suggestion that heaven is not merely *above* man. Because regeneration, health, or perfection depends on the circulatory process of rising and falling, heaven must include what is *below* man, too, as a part of the dynamic constituting the whole. By *below* Emerson means the depths of the human heart; heaven is what men "inwardly aspire after" (W, II, 140): "the heaven predicted from the beginning of the world" is "still predicted from the bottom of the heart" (W, II, 140). One's fall, therefore, should be into the region of the heart so that he might, paradoxically, rise from there to the realm of heaven.

This circulatory pattern underlies the remark that one "speaks the truth in the spirit of truth"—that is, one produces "the flower and head of all living nature" (W, II, 166)—when "his eye is as clear as the heavens" (W, II, 156). By *eye* Emerson means not only the external eye which brings images inward but also the internal eye which perceives spiritual reality through phenomena. The word *heavens* in this passage, then, refers to the external skies *above* man perceived by the physical eye as well as to the internal celestial vistas *within* man detected by the inner eye.

Both manners of perception are interrelated in the circulatory process of the universe; and finally both acts of vision, near and far, are inseparably joined. The action of the will integrates all extremities, such as lower and upper. In action, as Emerson's customary reliance on images of labor suggests, the will functions like a heart to perpetuate the circulatory process and to maintain the ceaseless transition between falling and rising. These genuine actions of the will reveal that heaven lies above *and* within man, that "there is a soul at the centre of nature and over the will of every man" (W, II, 139). Man is bathed inside and outside by the circulation of the One Man, in whom he serves as an organ.

The image of man as an organ bathed externally and internally by the circulation of the One Man naturally suggested to Emerson the applicability of respiration to his hieroglyph, for breathing is a form of circulation dependent on the incessant rise and fall of the lungs. Referring to "the obedient spiracle" of one's character (W, II, 142), Emerson not only suggests an opening (spiracle) which allows external air to bathe man internally in the process of breathing, but also plays on the word *spiral* and specifically on the heavenly *aspiration* of the heart which rises by falling even as the physical heart pulses blood or the lungs circulate air. Emerson makes this image of the spiracle specific, perhaps almost too concrete, when he coalesces the image of the windpipe with the more mundane image of pipes which conduct water. The will of the great man is an "obedient spiracle" in the sense that it is like a "smooth and hollow" pipe; thus the will provides "an unobstructed channel" for the circulating water of the universe—the image may have been suggested by the first chapter of Genesis— water which completes its circuit by falling so that finally it always "rises to the level of its source" (W, II, 134, 137).

As the image of circulation implies, man is, even as a pipe, bathed internally as well as externally by the universal water. He possesses a "fluid consciousness" and is surrounded by "fluid events" (W, II, 138, 148). To achieve a proper rhythm between these two facets of his being, he should exercise his will so as to place himself "in the middle of the stream of power and wisdom which animates all" (W, II, 139). This is a subtly difficult statement, not in the original version of the present long passage (EL, III, 281); its real sense is revealed only in light of the motif under discussion. The placement of oneself "in the middle of the stream of power and wisdom" suggests the image of a healthy organ (man) fully supplied by circulating fluids. But the word *animates* alerts the reader to the soul (*anima*) at his center, which in turn suggests that he should place himself completely at the center of his own being or self. This implication makes sense, of course, when it is realized that the universal water circulates within as well as outside the One Man, that heaven lies inside as well as above each individual, and that what is internal in the soul of man is identical to what is external in the Over-Soul of the One Man.

In this context, substantially revising the original comment (JMN, VIII, 62), Emerson remarks that one can measure the "depth of thought" by "how much water" it draws (W, II, 153). Thinking, as indicated in "The American Scholar," is the dynamic transition (will) between seeing (using the feet of the intellect) and speaking. In "Spiritual Laws" he makes the same point when he explains thought's water-like influx as something which will "lift you from your feet with the great voice of eloquence" (W, II, 153).

This rise and subsequent fall is an aspect of the oscillating principle of life. When the will is an "obedient spiracle," it participates "on the waves of its love and hope"; then it "can uplift all that is reckoned solid and precious in the world" (W, II, 165). By this Emerson means that everything is buoyed spirally upward in the current of the aspiration of the heart (similar to the lung's respiration) wherein lies "a deepening channel into an infinite sea" (W, II, 141). Thus the universal water slowly rises to its source. Anyone who possesses such a will or heart provides "the blood in our proper veins" (W, II, 150). Through such a person, others discover that in their own pipes—in their own veins, arteries, and windpipes (physical and spiritual)—flow the currents of life; through him, they realize that the rhythm of the universe as an organism (the One Man) is identical to their own rhythm as an organ, that "the stream is blood" (W, II, 155).

Emerson incorporates other ancillary features within this central image of circulation. For instance, he includes a book motif. A true book, which ultimately (like nature) is the text provided by the lives of great men, always participates in this rhythmic rise and fall of life. Only those books which are kept in "circulation" manage to "come down" to us (W, II, 154); only those books which "fall" to each successive generation share in the oscillatory principle of nature and thereby rise to endure. This continual circulation of great books is guaranteed by the fact that: "never was a sincere word utterly lost. Never a magnanimity *fell* to the ground, but there is some *heart* to greet and accept it unexpectedly" (W, II, 158–59; italics added). Every word "falls" to the heart of each generation, where it is renewed and pumped upward again. In other words, as Emerson's coalesced images suggest, every word "falls" to each generation as if it were ripe fruit, the seeds of which (through the dynamic of the renewing heart or will) "give rise" to a new thought, a new "flower and head" (W, II, 166). Indeed, by means of this process of obedient receptivity or "lowly listening" one "shall hear the right word" (W, II, 139); and through participation in this natural undulation "the mind is ripened" (W, II, 147). All magnanimities (greatnesses of soul) fall like ripe fruit because they "have their weight" (W, II, 145). Emerson, of course, is punning on the meaning of *weight* as commodity and, to the more perceptive mind, as significance or value (images of value also comprise a motif). The weight of a book, in the sense of its worth, proves crucial to its partaking in the rise-and-fall circulatory principle of nature. In this regard, "Spiritual Laws" instructs the reader to beware misassessment of nature's rhythm by an "over-estimate" (too high) or an "under-estimate" (too low), to avoid a mistaken "worship of magnitude" (W, II, 165, 161) based on a sense of commodity rather than on a higher, more spiritual reality.

Emerson's ideal man places himself, therefore, between the high and the low extremities of nature's currents, which bathe him internally and externally. This means that his will remains

ever-active, always engaged in the dynamic of falling and rising or in the transition between seeing (lower extremity) and
speaking (upper extremity). The great man is like the great
book: always in circulation. In "Spiritual Laws"—although, as
we shall see, "Self-Reliance" presents the motif somewhat
more cleverly—Emerson depicts this condition as a sleeping
man who (like a fallen fruit) must eventually awaken and rise.
Both positions are aspects of the tree that is man and the larger
fruit-bearing tree of life of which he is a branch: "Action and
inaction are alike to the true. One piece of the tree is cut for a
weathercock [upper extremity of standing] and one for the
sleeper of a bridge [lower extremity of reclining]; the virtue of
the wood is apparent in both" (W, II, 162).[17]

This sense of the ceaseless unity of rising and falling in man
and of the expectancy he should feel as a result is communicated in the opening paragraph of "Spiritual Laws" when Emerson remarks that "the infinite lies stretched in smiling repose"
(W, II, 132). Successive awakenings or risings comprise man's
destiny, not only in general but in particular, because even
(and perhaps especially) he who functions as the "lowest organ" is bathed in "the highest love" of the current of being
(W, II, 160). The blood or being of the universe circulates
through the ever-widening, ascending channels made by the
dynamic art of the aspiring godlike heart. Circulation is the
One Man, the deity beyond any other definition than the expression "I AM" (W, II, 160).

Appropriately the hieroglyph of the One Man in "Spiritual
Laws" never quite condenses into concrete visibility. Although
every motif in the essay helps convey a visual impression of the
hieroglyph to the inner eye of the reader, the central ordering
image finally remains as elusive as the end toward which the
upward spiral of human aspiration and of the universal circulation asymptotically approaches.

In "The Over-Soul"

In "Compensation," "The Over-Soul," and "Circles" (all
1841) Emerson moved away from his image of circulation in

the One Man toward the geometric circle, another hieroglyph of which he was fond.

In light of other writings in *Essays: First Series,* "Compensation" is not very interesting aesthetically,[18] and "Circles" merely makes vaguer use of motifs developed in "The Over-Soul." Critics have been properly sensitive to the relation between content and form in "Circles." Indeed, critical commentary on this essay is quite fine, especially when it relates Emerson's style to his meaning.[19] In my opinion, however, the utter apparentness of the geometric-circle motif weakens the essay so much that what it gains in lucidity it loses in artistry. Although sufficiently self-contained regarding its central hieroglyph, the work presents shards of imagery not derived from its internal integrity. Contrary to the conclusion of one critic that "Circles" functions as the nuclear essay,[20] it in fact depends on motifs established and developed in other essays in the first-series volume, especially in "The Over-Soul."

"The Over-Soul" depicts the individual heart as a microcosm of "the heart of being" or the One Man (W, II, 293). This "common heart" is "that Unity, that Over-Soul, within which every man's particular being is contained and made one with all other[s]" (W, II, 268). Men feel the "pulsation" of this heart as spontaneous inspiration or "impulse": "With each divine impulse the mind rends the thin rinds of the visible and finite, and comes out into eternity, and inspires and expires its air" (W, II, 275). As this imagery of respiration and circulation suggests, Emerson is using the hieroglyph of the One Man, particularly as he developed it in "Spiritual Laws."

Emerson is less interested in circulation than in its circular pattern as the central hieroglyph of "The Over-Soul" essay. Initially he presents the circle figure as pertaining to the realm of forms, of dream disguises, of "limitations that circumscribe" man (W, II, 272). An equivalent image is that of the obscuring "veil which curtains events" but which can be easily rent: "the web of events is the flowing robe" which clothes the soul (W, II, 284, 274; cf. the original version of the latter remark, EL, III, 39). Truth, however, does abide in this dreamlike veiled world of delusion; for "dreams, wherein often we see ourselves in masquerade," are merely "droll disguises only magnifying and enhancing the real element and forcing it on our distant notice" (W, II, 270). Behind the dreamlike veil of circumscribing limitation lies the truth that in reality "the soul circumscribes all things" (W, II, 272). If the human soul is a microcosm of the Over-Soul, as Emerson claims, then it is encircled only by itself and therefore is free from any ring of phenomenal limitations.

To see the truth of this ultimate circle, one must look within and "speak from within the veil" (W, II, 287); he must "come from [his] remote station on the circumference instantaneously to the centre of the world" (W, II, 276). Within the self, one detects the principle of outward expansion which dissolves the grip of the circle of forms on man's comprehension of life and which simultaneously engenders insight into the nature of the farthest circle of the Over-Soul. Emerson intentionally chooses the term *circumference* in reference to the phenomenal world, for it implies an imaginary circumscription, readily contractable or expandable. In the delusive world of forms, a circumference is all one has and it may be changed even as one can draw ever-larger circles with a compass. The point around which these expanding circles are generated is the self, from whence insight is derived. "From within or from behind, a light shines through us upon things," Emerson explains, later remarking similarly that "the Maker of all things and all persons stands behind us and casts his dread omniscience through us over things" (W, II, 270, 280). By looking inward, then, one really looks outward; and whatever comes from within also must bear the truth of divine omniscience. Consequently, even in trivial conversations something "higher in each of us overlooks [in the double sense of ignores and surveys] this by-play, and Jove nods to Jove from behind each of us" (W, II, 278). "Attaining to a higher self-possession" (W, II, 277)—that is, achieving more advanced modes of selfhood—depends on recognizing the unity between the inner circle of self and the outer circle of the Over-Soul. To attain selfhood one must dissolve the delusion of a fixed circumference of phenomena and must discard the obscuring imaginary veil, a point Emerson humorously reiterates when he declares that nothing can "make you one of the circle, but the casting aside your trappings" (W, II, 291).

In "The Over-Soul" Emerson presents another feature of the One Man hieroglyph which functions correspondingly with images of the circle and of the veil: depiction of man as a building. He resorts to the traditional Christian notion of man as a temple of the Holy Spirit, not to his later portrayal in "Politics" of the One Man as an ascending defensive structure. However, as is so typical, he refashions the convention in a most original manner. He explains, "A man is the façade of a temple wherein all wisdom and all good abide" (W, II, 270–71). A façade is merely the face of a building, frontage through which one passes. Corresponding to the circumference line and the veil, the image serves as a sort of covert pun concerning the false face which circumstances put on in the dreamlike world of delusive phenomena. Emerson's point is that, in penetrating the veil and in recognizing the arbitrariness of a circumference line, one repudiates the claim to reality asserted by his own physical being in its engagement with phenomena. One must pass through the façade (frontal structure or masquerading delusion) of his own phenomenal being to the interior of the heart, where thought "arches . . . like a temple" (W, II, 277). Put another way, men are like the homes of certain Arabian sheiks which "affect an external poverty" and "reserve all their display of wealth for their interior" (W, II, 278–79).

The temple does not lie solely within, for what one encounters within is the principle of expansion leading to the truth of the ultimate circle, which is the Over-Soul. Thus, just as the circle can be within or beyond an arbitrary circumference, the temple of which man is merely a façade (a circumference or veil) lies outwardly as well as inwardly, though man has access only in terms of the latter. Like the heart which it is, this temple possesses "chambers" (W, II, 267); but just as the self (a microcosm of the Over-Soul) is infinite, the temple of man's interior, like that which contains the Over-Soul, is not confined by walls or limitations. Thus Emerson says, "We lie open on one side to the deeps of spiritual nature" (W, II, 272). When one has penetrated to the center of his own being, to the center of the temple, "the Deity will shine through him, through all the disguises . . . of unfavorable circumstance" (W, II, 286–87). The disguises represented by the façade, veil, rind, circumference, or delusion of the phenomenal world will disappear. Such externals will give way to the internal home of God, the source of a proper architecture for man's thoughts.

Emerson's development of the notion of the heart as the temple of the Deity clarifies the sense in which every heart is a microcosm of the macrocosmic heart of the One Man. Again, as in "Spiritual Laws," the image of the blood's circulation conveys the dynamics of this union: "the heart in thee is the heart of all; not a valve, not a wall, not an intersection is there anywhere in nature, but one blood rolls uninterruptedly an endless circulation through all men, as the water of the globe is all one sea, and, truly seen, its tide is one" (W, II, 294). Throughout "The Over-Soul," water symbolizes the relation of the human heart to the One Man. In a remark derived from an early lecture entitled "Holiness" (EL, II, 343) and inserted in a passage drawn from another early essay entitled "Doctrine of the Soul" (EL, III, 14), Emerson says, "Man is a stream whose source is hidden" (W, II, 268). In the chambers of the temple of the heart man can detect this "ethereal water," an "ebb of the individual rivulet before the flowing surges of the sea of life," the "tide of being which floats us into the secret of nature," the "influx" of the "universal self" (W, II, 268, 281, 284, 292). "The Over-Soul" is replete with such imagery and stresses that genius results from "a larger imbibing of the common heart" (W, II, 288).

As my opening remarks on "The Over-Soul" suggest, Emerson associates this circulatory influx or impulse from the divine heart with respiration, even as he did in "Spiritual Laws." In "The Over-Soul," however, he develops another related pattern based on the image of fire or light. When he speaks of a "sea of light" and of a celestial fire "which burns until it shall dissolve all things into the waves and surges of an ocean of light" (W, II, 290, 285), Emerson prepares the reader for a motif based on light which will parallel the water motif in its symbolic function. Light, like water and air, evidences the principle of circulation between the human and the divine heart. In fact, the human heart or soul is light (W, II, 270), the principle of animation in every organ (man) of the One Man; it follows that the true thought of the soul "shines for all" (W, II, 277). Genuine thoughts and actions, "the faintest glow of virtuous emotion, in which form it warms, like our household fires" (W, II, 281), can prevail only when the temple of the heart is inhabited by the Deity, when "God fire[s] the heart with his presence" (W, II, 292).

As these observations suggest, the One Man hieroglyph functions much more recessively in "The Over-Soul" than in "The American Scholar," "Politics," and "Spiritual Laws." Apparently Emerson meant to reduce specificity of the hieroglyph as well as of other favorite, related imagery. When a hieroglyph threatened to become too concrete, he lessened detail even while maintaining an overall design. As a result, the reader is unable to grasp the image at the level of the Understanding without frustration: from his "distant notice" he is unable to focus clearly on the elusive image. Although he perceives something subliminally, his conscious mind cannot come to terms with the image any more than it can cope—however conventional the images may be—with the paradox of fire and water serving as correlatives. Specificity of images dissolves before conscious pursuit, disappears in the circulatory sweep of Emerson's prose. Like the soul, which looks steadily forward "creating a world before her, leaving worlds behind her" (W, II, 274), Emerson, as the prophet of the soul, creates and dissolves his images. The "soul's communication of truth" in words "is the highest event in nature" (W, II, 280).

In the healthy circulatory process of nature, events give way to new events; specificity of event or image gives way to circulation, to the fluid process whereby the circle is infinitely contractable and expandable. Through the circulation of Emerson's prose emerges a tide "which floats us into the secret of nature." The hieroglyphs of his essays briefly burn until they dissolve "into the waves and surges of an ocean of light." The reader *approaches*, in a mystical manner, the attainment of a flash of insight into the deity who is the One Man and who, albeit greater than any individual, somehow also abides in the temple of the individual heart—that deity who is pure, blinding light and hence always beyond vision.

III

The Traveling Geologist Hieroglyph

In "Experience"

E xperience" (1844) is artistically one of the most complex
essays and consequently one of the most difficult to expli-
cate. It is rich not only in regard to the significant adjustment
Emerson was making concerning human limitation, as Stephen
Whicher has cogently demonstrated,[1] but also in terms of his
artistic development. Emerson, it is fair to speculate, channeled
some emotional strain of this time of change into his art, with
the result that his art benefited from the early stages of his
personal crisis. In some subtle way artistic control or discipline
may have provided Emerson with a means of confronting his
increasing skepticism after the emotional loss he sustained from
the death of his son Waldo in 1842. The aesthetic design of
"Experience" argues, even better than its explicit remarks, for a
principle of order beneath the seeming chaos of life's events.

The pivotal hieroglyph in "Experience" is the planet earth.[2]
At the simplest level Emerson focuses on symbolic features of
the two extreme regions, the Frigid and the Torrid Zones.
Throughout the essay he imaginatively equates the human
head with the polar areas. Frequently, in this context, he applies images suggesting coldness to the geometry, calculation,
design, and skepticism of the intellect, the source of science.
The region of the Equator, in contrast, serves as an equivalent
for man's feet. Developing his earlier association of this part
of the human anatomy with instinct in "The American Scholar,"
Emerson appropriately attributes impulse, spontaneity, expec-

tation, and piety—all of which are frequently associated in the essay with imagery suggesting heat—to the feet of man and to the Torrid Zone of earth, symbolizing the origin of the force of religion. These extremes, Emerson explains, constitute the law of nature. In nature "everything runs to excess" (W, III, 65–66). But since every excess has its natural antithesis, opposites always ultimately function to create a new dynamically unified balance. The skepticisms of science, consequently, merely prove to be "limitations of the affirmative statement" of religion (W, III, 75), and vice versa. The "ardors of piety agree at last with the coldest skepticism" (W, III, 69).

Referring to these two extremities Emerson explains that one "may climb into the thin and cold realm of pure geometry and lifeless science, or sink into that of sensation" (W, III, 62). Although experience seems to necessitate that man live in one region or the other—and significantly he stresses the coldness of skeptical distance as the most prevalent choice— ideally Temperate Zones do exist. "The middle region of our being is the temperate zone," and here, in contrast to the extreme Equator of the Torrid Zone, lies the real equalizer or "equator of life" (W, III, 62).

The existence of this world scheme is, Emerson admits, a mystery, its cause ineffable. Several early philosophers tried to symbolize this cause in terms of the elements: "Thales by water, Anaximenes by air, . . . Zoroaster by fire" (W, III, 72–73). But, Emerson notes, these images are only metaphors, sundry synecdoches used to represent the whole. Imagistically combining all three elements in "Experience," he creates a still more encompassing metaphor for the inexplicable principle of life. Predictably he associates fire with the Torrid Zone, water with the Temperate Zone, and air with the Frigid Zone.

In "Experience," as in "The Over-Soul," Emerson associates these three elements with images of motion or flux. In both essays he prefers water (H_2O), which combines the extremes of fire (hydrogen) and air (oxygen) just as his correlative for water, the Temperate Zones, joins the Torrid Zone and the Frigid Zones. "All things swim" (W, III, 45), Emerson remarks in the opening paragraph. The person who is in sympathy with the scheme of things realizes that he is "a swimmer among drowning men" (W, III, 81). The average person, however, is unable to execute "direct strokes" because, in spite of his inundation, he possesses no internal waterlike flux, "no superfluity of spirit" (W, III, 49, 45).

Emerson extends the motif somewhat by depicting a person's life as a ship afloat on the waterlike flux of the world. "Every ship is a romantic object, except that we sail in" (W, III, 46); the problem is, Emerson explains, that "our life looks trivial" rather than "romantic" and that we are easily frustrated by "a tempest of fancies," by an "innavigable sea [which] washes with silent waves between us and the things we aim at" (W, III, 46, 60, 48). The "only ballast," he declares, "is a respect to the present hour" (W, III, 60; cf. III, 64).

Elsewhere in the essay this reference to the present hour is related to the central hieroglyph of the earth. Just as man ought ideally to dwell in a Temperate Zone, between the vertical extremes of the North or South Pole (skepticism) and the Equator (affirmation), so likewise he ought to live in the present, between the horizontal extremes of the past (East) and the future (West). Temperance should govern one's horizontal extremities, even as it should regulate his vertical tendencies, in spite of the fact that he is "ready to die out of nature and be born again into this new yet unapproachable America . . . found in the West" (W, III, 72). As Emerson indicates in this further instance of a specifically American metaphor,[3] East and West represent extremities of nature too and both prove necessary to the unitary promise signified by the eternal present. Living in the present, in the east-west cycle "of sunsets and sunrises every day" (W, III, 63), provides the ballast for equilibrium (the quoted phrase did not appear in the original version of the passage of which it is now a part [JMN, VIII, 285]).

Achieving ballast is one way to maintain a balance between the excesses of nature and of the human self. Balance is the thematic focus of "Experience."[4] In his delineation of nature's extremities Emerson includes the function of "power and form," which he associates respectively with the Torrid and the Frigid Zones. Between these aspects of life a "proportion must be invariably kept," he warns, for each "in excess makes a mischief" (W, III, 65). He suggests that ice-skating provides an appropriate metaphor for how one should effect this balance or proportion. According to his famous dictum in the essay, "we live amid surfaces, and the true art of life is to skate well on them" (W, III, 59). Without balance, without proportion between power and form, skating becomes disastrous; and this is precisely Emerson's point about a lack of balance with regard to human experience, symbolized by ice-skating.

Later in the essay when Emerson remarks that "experience is hands and feet to every enterprise" (W, III, 67), he plays on his metaphor of ice-skating and its implied idea of balance. But the comment also makes more evident that one is to attain this balance—the reference is sufficiently general to refer to skating, swimming, and boating, the three activities mentioned in relation to the foregoing remarks—through the coördination of both feet and hands. Emerson associates the feet with instinct and the hands with the will, just as he did in his development of the One Man hieroglyph. The will provides the dynamics for interaction between the lower extremity of instinct and the upper extremity of intellect; with regard to "Experience" the will is the source of any equipoise between the *power* of instinct (equivalent to the Torrid Zone and the feet) and the *form* of intellect (equivalent to the North or South Frigid Zone and the head).

Emerson is by no means as optimistic as he once was about human ability to use the will to attain balance. In the darker phase of his thinking represented by "Experience" he amply recognizes the obstacle implied by the frozen solidity of form and by the fire of power buried in man's unconscious regions: "Power keeps quite another road than the turnpikes of choice and will; namely the subterranean and invisible tunnels and channels of life" (W, III, 67). Nevertheless, for Emerson human dignity derives from exercise of the will, from interaction of intellect and instinct, in an endless effort to maintain equi-

librium on the "slippery sliding surfaces" of life to avoid letting
life "slip through our fingers" (W, III, 48, 49; the hand image
is intentional). Through exercise of the will one can struggle
to unite the extremes of his existence or, in terms of the essay's
central hieroglyph, "possess [his] axis more firmly" (W, III,
81).

Emerson consistently identifies the will as the locus of action. In "Experience" he frequently associates the will with
images of muscular activity, particularly, as the reader has
come to expect from earlier essays, with the use of hands.
Whereas, Emerson observes, many people possess hands "too
soft and tremulous for successful labor," a person "of native
force prospers . . . by skill of handling" (W, III, 59–60). The
former type has not learned that "intellectual tasting of life will
not supersede muscular activity" (W, III, 58). The intellect
alone or, for that matter, the feet alone prove insufficient in the
human encounter with experience. Principally the hands (the
will) are required in such encounters (symbolized in the activities of skating, swimming, and boating) if one is to achieve
balance or coordination between the head and the feet, between form and power.

Emerson extends his images of muscular activity and coördination to include those of journeying. "Experience" is replete with references to roads and traveling. Journeying requires
a careful balance between man's three principal extremities,
especially since "the line he must walk is a hair's breadth" (W,
III, 66). The successful traveler, the one who can "finish the
moment" or effect the balance of living in the present between
past (East) and future (West), will "find the journey's end in
every step of the road" (W, III, 60). This remark, clear enough
in itself, typifies Emerson's fondness for coalescing two motifs
by means of a simple play on words. In this instance the word
step refers not only to walking but also to the related matter of
climbing, an image Emerson identifies with the "ascending"
outcome of the muscular activity expended in journeying. Emerson utilizes the same technique when he observes that people
"stand on the brink of the ocean of thought and power, but

they never take the single step that would bring them there"
(W, III, 56–57). That is, people fail to participate in or on the
water of life where, through muscular activity (swimming,
boating, skating), they could strive to unite the extremities of
intellect and instinct, thereby advancing a step on the ascending stairway of life.

In the opening paragraph Emerson specifies the stair image:
"there are stairs below us, which we seem to have ascended;
there are stairs above us, many a one, which go upward and
out of sight" (W, III, 45). The top and bottom of this stairway
are equivalent to the extremities of man's being; man is to engage in the process of unending ascent, in the eternal dynamic
of transforming instinct upwardly into thought, by maintaining
a balance through the proper exercise of the coordinating hands
or will. This image of man balancing himself while ascending a
stairway is the most complex component of the hieroglyph in
"Experience" and one of the most poetically successful Emerson ever devised. By suggesting that man is himself the staircase to be climbed Emerson transcends classification, baffles
the Understanding, and conveys a brief visual impression, the
complex truth of which the reader can only intuitively glimpse.

Predictably the darker thinking reflected in "Experience"
dims optimism concerning this ascent. Although Emerson still
asserts that "the Ideal [is] journeying always with us" (W, III,
71), he is less certain about man's ability to achieve the requisite balance. Consequently, Emerson points to the average person's tendency to founder at sea, drown in the ocean, succumb
to the tempest, misstep on the stairway, stumble in the road,
and slip on the ice. The image of falling in "Experience" functions identically to that in "Spiritual Laws": every fall recapitu-
lates the significance of the myth of the primeval Fall, which
itself allegorizes "the discovery . . . that we exist" (W, III,
75). Although in the later essay ("Experience") he is less optimistic about these falls, Emerson still clearly sees them as potential *felices culpae* and readily concludes that "we thrive by
casualties" (W, III, 68). As the ambiguity of *casualty* suggests,
man develops or matures in terms of ordinary (casual) hap-

penings, chance accidents both good and bad, and misfortunes or falls. That one should thrive on ordinary occurrences as well as on mishaps is a typical Emersonian paradox. A fall preludes a subsequent rise, a belief informing Emerson's notion of the *felix culpa* presented in both "Spiritual Laws" and "Experience." The value of life does not entirely lie westward in the future, does not depend on knowing "what may *befall*" one (W, III, 53; italics added); rather it lies in the good and bad ordinary casualties or accidents which befall everyone in the immediate present, in the "series of surprises" which constitute life (W, III, 67). Each unexpected fall provides an opportunity for one to discover that he possesses being. The pain of a fall, if it does nothing else, at least awakens the victim to the fact that he is alive. Unfortunately for many, Emerson seriously jokes, such incidents merely occasion a time to *fall* asleep (W, III, 50).

Sleep characterizes man's inability to perceive his own existence. "Sleep lingers all our lifetime about our eyes," Emerson explains, and "dream delivers us to dream" (W, III, 45, 50). Significantly, in spite of the fact that the entire diurnal cycle contributes importantly to the scheme of "Experience," evening is the period of day most frequently stressed, just as autumn is the season most often implied. In the evening of man's current life, human sight becomes distorted, subject to "optical illusion[s]" (W, III, 52). The problem is that people "do not see directly, but mediately" (W, III, 75). The word *mediate* is two-edged in this instance. Explicitly it indicates that man's vision is limited by the *media* of air, fire, and water which constitute his environment; implicitly it points ironically to the fact that seeing directly, like executing "direct strokes," depends on ability to *mediate* between the extremities of being, to balance on the *middle* point represented by the present and by the Temperate Zones.

Man continually finds himself off center because he sees through "colored and distorting lenses" (W, III, 75). These lenses are not only the media of the elements but also the medium of the human eye; for the inner *I* that informs the human

eye is subject to temperament. Temperament, Emerson observes, "is the iron wire on which the beads [of moods which
"prove to be many-colored lenses"] are strung" (W, III, 50).
The beads or moods of temperament enclose man "in a prison
of glass" (W, III, 52).

A bead, an eye, or a glass lens is curved—a feature providing an image for the self and, as well, an ingenious way to relate these matters to the central hieroglyph of the Earth. The
curve of the eye or of the "crescive self" (W, III, 77),[5] like that
of the earth, represents the limits of necessity; the human self
is prone to be "too convex or too concave and cannot find a
focal distance within the actual horizon of human life" (W,
III, 51). Like the north-south poles and east-west horizons, the
human eye tends toward excessiveness. In fact "it is the eye
which makes the horizon" (W, III, 76), and whether that eye
is nearsighted or farsighted determines whether one tends more
or less toward the past or future (East-West) and toward skepticism or affirmation (Frigid Zones–Torrid Zone).

In terms of the controlling hieroglyph, "the rounding
mind's eye" (W, III, 76) and its horizon obscure the underside
of the planetary sphere and of the "crescive self." In a clever
development of the sphere image, Emerson notes that one lives
on a convex surface, the other side of which is a concave surface. This observation dissolves the apparent fixity of the human condition; for the world and the self are both convex and
concave, depending on how one views them. At the level of
intuitive perception the reader is to see how convexity becomes
concavity and vice versa, how finally the distinctions cancel
each other into some mysterious unity.

Emerson applies this image more complexly by suggesting
that the concave dome of the heavens is equivalent to the concave underside of the earth's surface. With this equation in
mind, he writes: "the new molecular philosophy shows astronomical interspaces betwixt atom and atom, shows that the
world is all outside; it has no inside" (W, III, 63–64). The
word *astronomical* pivotally intimates the relation between the
arc of the heavens and the myriads of arcs that comprise atomic

arrangements, including the layer of surface beneath man's feet, as merely another celestial-like dome arching over still another span ad infinitum. There exists, then, an astronomy above and below man. With regard to the arc of the eye, to which the earth's horizons correspond, there is an astronomy outside as well as inside the "crescive self." To look within the self is equivalent to looking beneath the earth's convex surface, only to discover further that within the self lies the same concave reality evident in the arc reflected in the heavens.

Thus, Emerson remarks: "Underneath the inharmonious and trivial particulars, is a musical perfection; the Ideal journeying always with us, the heaven without rent or seam" (W, III, 71). Heaven is below as well as above (as "Spiritual Laws" indicated). This point similarly is evident in the same paragraph when he again refers to the self's inner realm in terms of sky imagery and to an Edenic promised land regained: "this region gives further sign of itself, as it were in flashes of light, in sudden discoveries of its profound beauty and repose, as if the clouds that covered it parted at intervals and showed the approaching traveller the inland mountains, with the tranquil eternal meadows spread at their base, whereon flocks graze and shepherds pipe and dance" (W, III, 71). In this internal landscape of the self—the place of which Emerson earlier spoke as the sub*terranean* region and of which his central hieroglyph gives a brief flashing visual impression—lie the inland mountains of "reality, sharp peaks and edges of truth" (W, III, 67, 48).

The concave subterranean reality underlying man's convex surface existence is the realm of the unconscious. By associating the heavens above with this region Emerson not only makes excellent use of the astronomical motif but also conveys a sense of the essential unity underlying the apparent polarity in man's psychic terrain and in the earth's geographical zones. In this region of the underside of the convex self and of the planetary crust reside the fires of impulse which the feet, walking on the earth's surface, symbolize. In this region originates the "vast-flowing vigor" which "will fill up the vacancy between heaven and earth," the *"universal impulse to believe"* which balances skepticism, the essential "religious sentiment" which is independent of "the seasons of the year and the state of the blood" (W, III, 73, 74, 51).

This reference to circulation and the annual cycle, albeit pertinent to the arc imagery pervading the essay, bears witness to Emerson's changed perspective. Whereas in "History" (1841), he had written that "the hours should be instructed by the ages and the ages explained by the hours" (W, II, 4). In "Experience" only the former is true; Emerson does stress the importance of living in the present and of relishing every hour (W, III, 61); but he also indicates that "the years teach much which the days never know" (W, III, 69).

"Experience," in fact, emphasizes expanding circles. The limited diurnal cycle gives way to the annual cycle, which in turn yields to the lifetime. With the expansion of these circles of time comes a contingent expansion of horizons. All such expansion, however, occurs on an arc with a convex surface and a concave underside; this fact means that although expansion is indeed involved, progress is circular. In this sense of circularity, life is like a "kitten chasing so prettily her own tail" (W, III, 80). As man's perception of the arc that is his world and his self widens, "every object fall[s] successively into the subject itself" (W, III, 79), a comment relating the circle motif to the notion of *felices culpae*.

The genuine man explores the convex surface of the arc of earthlike self with the eyes of a prospector. For Emerson, it is primarily the artist who prospects, for he possesses *insight* (i.e., he digs beneath the convex surface, the underside of which is equivalent to the inner self) as well as *foresight* (i.e., he sees beyond the convex surface of limitation outward toward the concave reality of the heavenly dome which parallels the underside of earthlike self).

The great man, therefore, is "like a travelling geologist who passes through our estate and shows us good slate, or limestone, or anthracite, in our brush pasture" (W, III, 80). He is a geologist in the sense that, as a student of the earth, he sees in the terrene landscape an image of the inner self. He travels in the sense that he exerts balancing muscular activity in his explorations which expand man's assessment of the art of his world and his life. The great man assesses the human "estate," a word which nicely incorporates the double implication of geological imagery throughout "Experience" by referring simultaneously to one's *land* and to one's *condition*. As the imagery indicates, the great man reveals the subterranean value of man's landscape/condition hidden beneath the illusory surface of human existence. The "inland mountains," the region of "sharp peaks and edges of truth," serves as his domain; and through the muscular activity of his exploration he discovers that "man is like a bit of Labrador spar, which has no lustre as you turn it in your hand until you come to a particular angle" (W, III, 71, 48, 57). Unlike the illusory precision of scientific report, observations of the great man or poet focus on the elusive meaning of his exploration; for the arc of the world and of the self on which he conducts his investigations is nonending (as object forever becomes subject) with the consequence that "the results of life are uncalculated and uncalculable" (W, III, 69). But the traveling geologist's perspective or creative eye expands the horizons of the circular terrain of human existence. In this sense the "promises to western roads" and the "passage into new worlds," particularly to the "yet unapproachable America" (W, III, 58, 85, 72), are realized through the muscular activity of the traveling geologist who discloses the value of the present.

Emerson, it is no surprise to note, identifies with the image of the traveling geologist. As an artist he asserts his will and hands in muscular activity by creating the central hieroglyph of "Experience" in order to give a flashing impression of the interior wealth of the human estate. This image and its related motifs, always elusively flickering at the periphery of the reader's mental vision, are like the Labrador spar which must be held at a certain angle before its luster can be perceived. The geological and geographical imagery of "Experience" glitters similarly every time Emerson reveals the inherent and hidden dimension beneath its mundane reality—the strange relation between concave and convex surfaces, the ambiguity of the word *estate*, the human analogy implicit in the planetary sphere, for by now obvious examples. Emerson uses imagery prospectively; he discovers the subterranean value of the image (insight) and discloses that wealth in flashes of illumination which expand his reader's vision of the mundane and sense of horizon (foresight). By using images derived from nature's landscape in this manner, Emerson mines the inland mountains or subterranean regions of the human self.

Because the self is "crescive," like eye lens and earth curvature, in Emerson's view the artist cannot provide any permanent answers. On the arc he travels he encounters the obstructive "lords of life" (illusion, temperament, succession, surface, surprise, reality, and subjectivity—all objectified by imagery already discussed), and, more significantly, an endless circle of discoveries. This fact that the artist cannot give permanent answers applies as well to the inland truth revealed through the central hieroglyph: "I know better than to claim any completeness of my picture. I am a fragment, and this is a fragment of me" (W, III, 83).

The elusiveness of Emerson's hieroglyph, then, approximates aesthetically not only the experience of the dimly perceived future prospects looming on man's horizon (West) but also the experience of the dimly beheld fact slipping away into the past (East). The illuminating central image of an essay should be as spontaneous as the artist can make it; its elusive brevity then emphasizes the present moment, which (like the media of water, air, and fire) is always in flux between the horizontal extremities of past and future. Such artistry, in which "there must not be too much design," instructs that "the art of life has a pudency" or modesty of proportion (W, III, 68–69). This point, it should be recalled, is emphasized in "Experience": the need for balance between the vertical and horizontal excesses to which man, nature, and art are prone. Aesthetically Emerson tries to communicate this through an image which, in its elusive specificity, combines calculation and instinct, the past and the future. The shimmering hiero-glyph, product of the muscular activity of Emerson's self, ap-propriately dramatizes the organizing yet fluid dynamic of the intermediating will uniting extremities of the self (head/feet) in the immediacy of the present moment.

As the reader experiences this seemingly concrete yet elu-sive hieroglyph, he finds himself "at sea," swimming among images as shimmery and illusory as the surfaces of life from which they are drawn. This engagement of the reader is what Emerson spoke of as creative reading in "The American Scholar." The dynamic coordinating activity of the reader's will struggles for balance amidst the swirl of the fluid sentences and their seemingly scattered images, all mysteriously impart-ing a collective visual impression of a vaguely unified hiero-glyph. In "Experience" Emerson suggests that the reader should be a prospector; like the artist, he should see *into* and *beyond* art, nature, and the self: "Nature and books belong to the eyes that see them" (W, III, 50). His hieroglyphs embody what should be seen, possessed, and eventually transcended.

The fullness of my preceding discussion, my attempt to indicate the interrelatedness of the imagery in "Experience," should suggest the high aesthetic achievement of the essay.

I have not mentioned, however, still other related, though minor, motifs in the work; rather I have focused on and inte-grated major features of the central hieroglyph. Like the image of the One Man, the images of the earth and of man as a traveling geologist and geographer appear time and again in Emerson's writings.

In "Nature"

In some earlier version "Nature" (1844) was probably the essay Emerson had intended to include in *Essays: First Series* (see JMN, VII, 498). In its present form, however, the work suits *Essays: Second Series*, especially since it develops the central hieroglyph in "Experience." The essay merits close scru-tiny despite the derivation of its controlling image because it provides a fascinating example of how Emerson managed other facets of a hieroglyph. In "Nature" the planetary sphere provides the central image, but its rotation is the feature which now interests Emerson: "Given the planet, it is still necessary to add the impulse" (W, III, 185). In "Nature," in fact, Emerson explains what he tried to do whenever he revised a motif. The comment reads: "the artist still goes back for materials and begins again with the first elements on the most advanced stage" (W, III, 181). A hieroglyph ought to advance as the vision from which it was derived in the artist did and as the insight which it conveys to the reader should.

Initially the reappearance of the sphere hieroglyph seems unpromising. Once again Emerson notes the correspondence between man and earth, particularly concerning the Polar and Torrid Zones. He equates the human head with the Polar regions, which symbolize the principle of identity in nature and man. This principle is "*natura naturata,* or nature passive" (W, III, 176) and concerns the delusive features of form, fixity, and rest which people erroneously designate as reality. Human feet, on the contrary, correspond to the Torrid Zone, symbol of the principle of motion in man and nature. This principle is "Efficient Nature, *natura naturans,* the quick cause before which all forms flee" (W, III, 179); it pertains, in direct contrast to identity, to metamorphosis, fluidity, and action.

Emerson acknowledges that insofar as identity and motion interact they cannot be construed as antagonists. Rather they merely represent two chief components of a unitary dynamic. Just as the universe is comprised of "one stuff with its two ends" (W, III, 181), the zonal extremities of the earth are more related than antagonistic: "A little heat, that is a little motion, is all that differences the bald, dazzling white and deadly cold poles of the earth from the prolific tropical climates" (W, III, 179). The truth underlying this union of the two extremes can sometimes be directly experienced, as, for instance, during Indian Summer, when in spite of the fact that one lives in the "bleak upper sides of the planet" he basks for the moment "in the shining hours of Florida and Cuba" (W, III, 169). This interraction with its implied unitary dynamic is, of course, true for man's extremities as well. Man cannot help but polarize at times toward one extremity or the other, Emerson cautions. Indeed even "men of thought and virtue sometimes had the *head*ache, or wet *feet,* or could lose good time whilst the room was getting *warm* in *winter* days" (W, III, 191; italics added).

Throughout "Nature" Emerson refers to the winter and summer extremes which the Temperate Zones experience. This seasonal cycle comprises "the immortal year" (W, III, 170), the eternal interplay between identity and motion evident in the earth's revolution around the sun. The diurnal cycle, resulting from the earth's rotation around its axis, is even more prominent in the essay. Images of sunrise and sunset give a distinct impression of the dynamic unification of extremes. Day corresponds to the Torrid Zone; in the heat of the day men participate in a seemingly chaotic swirl of particulars. Like the child, whose immature stage parallels present human existence, man "lies down at night overpowered by the fatigue which this day of continual pretty madness has incurred" (W, III, 186); "after every foolish day we sleep off the fumes and furies of its hours" (W, III, 195). The dreams of the polar night prove just as real as the dreams of one's torrid daylight life and merely represent an opposite extreme participating in a mutual underlying unity. Proportion, Emerson makes clear, is requisite to an integration of activity and rest, a balance between extremities attained by a dynamic transition ever-prevalent in nature and, through the interaction of the will, ever-potential in man. Because this principle of dynamic unity or balance is reflected in the horizons of great paintings, such works of art appeal to us: "it is the magical lights of the horizon [night] and the blue sky [day] for the background which save all our works of art, which were otherwise bawbles" (W, III, 174). Presumably, in Emerson's opinion, the depiction of the dynamic unity symbolized in the diurnal cycle also characterizes great essays.

For man, who "carries the world in his head" (W, III, 183), the diurnal and seasonal cycles expressed in art as well as in nature communicate hope. They indicate he is not a slave to the external conditions in which he finds himself but rather he is the master of those conditions to the extent that "nature is the incarnation of a thought, and turns to a thought again, as ice becomes water and gas" (W, III, 196). Moreover, the very images of metamorphosis which man witnesses in this depiction of his mind evidence that he is no slave to any interior extremity. Indeed, "the world is mind precipitated [passive form], and the volatile essence [active fluidity] is forever escaping again into the state of free thought" (W, III, 196). Hope lies in this process whereby man projects outwardly into nature, giving rise to precipitation of identity or form, which in turn rebounds toward its source, giving rise to volatile motion or change—a new thought which will begin the process again. This is the principle of rotation, equivalent to the diurnal cycle, as it functions in the human self. By this process men "traverse the whole scale of being, from the centre to the poles of nature, and have some stake in every possibility" (W, III, 195–96). If the seasonal cycle is immortal, so is that of man's internal revolution. In the immortality of that process—one of expanding horizons of thought—lies human hope.

The optimism underlying this hope is qualitatively less intense and oracular than in Emerson's earlier writings. Whereas in *Nature* he had proclaimed that everything in the world is knowable, in "Nature" he indicates that the ultimate design of the universe, in spite of the fact that it is a creation of man's mind, will always exceed human comprehension. Such a notion, of course, comports with Emerson's idea of mankind's infinite upward ascendancy; but in "Nature" the image he devises to suggest the eternal dynamic of man's rotation between the extremities of identity and motion certainly intimates an element of frustration. This image, another feature of the sphere hieroglyph in the essay, depicts man as someone who reaches for the horizon by trying to stand on a ball. Who can go where the horizon lies, Emerson asks, "or lay his hand or plant his foot thereon? Off they fall from the round world forever and ever" (W, III, 193).

Correspondent to this image is the portrait of man as an expectant bridegroom about to marry the other part of himself reflected in the horizon. Man is the groom, the old bachelor, the lover, seeking "in marriage . . . felicity and perfection"; but the "betrothed lover has lost the wildest charm of his maiden in her acceptance of him. She was heaven whilst he pursued her as a star: she cannot be heaven if she stoops to such a one as he" (W, III, 178, 182, 187, 193). In this last passage the image of the star, Emerson's symbol for "spiritual magnificence" (W, III, 176), contributes to the bridegroom and the man-on-the-ball motifs. The stars, the nightly lights functioning as the counterpart of the sun, represent the horizon always extending beyond man's grasp, as we saw in Emerson's remark about great paintings. The stars betoken the "secret promises" (W, III, 174) of the spirit even as does the rainbow, the Biblical symbol of God's covenant with man. Nature, Emerson explains, "vaults like the fresh rainbow into the deep, but no archangel's wing was yet strong enough to follow it and report of the return of the curve"; for "nature converts itself into a vast promise, and will not be rashly explained" (W, III, 193–94).

The curve of the rainbow or the promise of the spirit disappears into the horizon, that same horizon for which the expectant bridegroom or the man-on-the-ball reaches. Faith in a law of proportion in nature counters man's continual frustration, a belief that "the drag is never taken from the wheel. Wherever the impulse exceeds, the Rest or Identity insinuates its compensation" (W, III, 194–95). The equalizing forces involved in this dynamic between the extremes of matter and spirit, identity and motion, prove salutary for man—a notion likewise evident in the religious writings of several seventeenth-century poets who viewed certain excesses as purgatives leading to health. Referring to this health-giving dynamic uniting the extremes of nature Emerson remarks, "All over the wide fields of earth grows the prunella or self-heal" (W, III, 195).

In a passage cited earlier in our discussion of correlation between the zones of the earth and human extremities, Emerson depicts polarization in man as an illness (headache) or as a

situation which may lead to an illness (wet feet). Wet feet or
dampened instinct can lead to a headache or distorted thought
—both are aspects of illness. Health requires the engagement
of "eyes and hands and feet" (W, III, 171). "What health,
what affinity!" Emerson exclaims over this condition of "firm
water" (i.e., the union of form and flux) and "cold flame" (i.e.,
the union of the Polar and Torrid Zones of the self) (W, III,
171). *Affinity* suggests not only one's nearness to the horizon
but also one's alliance through marriage. Perfect health, then,
depends on man's marriage to the elusive bride symbolized by
the equally elusive lights in the horizon. The "magical lights of
the horizon and the blue sky" in nature and in art symbolize
"enchantments [which] are medicinal" (W, III, 174, 171).

In his present state, however, "man is fallen" (W, III, 178);
consequently he is horizontal rather than vertical, ill from wet
feet and headache resulting from polarization. In contrast and
thus in aid to fallen man, medicinal "nature is erect, and serves
as a differential thermometer" (W, III, 178). At present, health
and marriage elude man, as well as the harmony (another recurrent motif in the essay) evinced in a good marriage and in
good health. Observing that "when we are convalescent, nature
will look up to us," Emerson reiterates his faith that "a benefi-
cent purpose lies in wait for us" (W, III, 178, 194). Health,
then, is equivalent to balancing one's self between extremes.
Even though the union of the two antitheses of identity and
motion can never be consummated, man achieves dignity by
pursuing this ideal expectantly.

Although the image of man as an expectant bridegroom
who never succeeds in marrying his ideal does not contradict
the image of man maintaining a healthy balance, some tension
persists. In actuality the tension lies in Emerson, pinpointing
the difference between his former faith in human potentiality
and his current, more darkly colored notion of human limitations. An earlier Emerson would have seen the healthy activity
of balancing as a consummation leading to further degrees of
union and of human dignity. The Emerson reflected in "Nature" sees human dignity originating from one's attempt to

stand erect in the midst of endless frustration. To be sure, the dynamic in which man engages in the latter instance still produces the same sort of spiral evolution implied by the former, and so man advances as thought gives way to thought. But the context of this growth has changed, for now Emerson admits that "there is throughout nature something mocking, something that leads us on and on, but arrives nowhere; keeps no faith with us" (W, III, 189–90). Man, the ever-expectant bride-groom, should maintain his faith. The fact that he cannot complete the arc of the rainbow, that every end is "prospective of some other end, which is also temporary; a round and final success nowhere" (W, III, 190), allows, in Emerson's view, for a human development and dignity supplanting any sense of frustration the system seems to warrant.

The image of a man trying to stand on a ball unintentionally undercuts, to some degree, the dignity of the human struggle for balance. Such imagery, unlike that used in "Experience," makes man seem somewhat foolish, as if he were engaged in a juvenile preoccupation. Moreover, Emerson clearly recognizes that no one can stand on the rotating planetary ball for long; man must continually fall off it, lie on his back convalescing, and rise to try again. In the last analysis, for man, balance remains as fleeting an experience as does the consummation of marriage to his ideal. The very process of falling and rising—or of pursuit (in terms of the marriage motif)—corresponds to the diurnal cycle of sunset and sunrise. Unwittingly Emerson's image may convey a more vivid impression of the pathetic than of the ennobling. But at the explicit level, for Emerson at least, human dignity emerges from "this immense sacrifice of men" (W, III, 192).

In "Uses of Great Men"

Whereas in "Nature" Emerson chiefly extends the zonal images of the hieroglyph of the planetary sphere presented in "Experience," in "Uses of Great Men" (1850) he primarily develops the related image of the traveling geologist and geographer who explores the earth and discovers passages into new worlds. In its simplicity this too-often-neglected essay imparts its hieroglyph much more readily than does either of the other two works. A careful reading, along the lines I have been demonstrating, suggests why John Albee found a "complete revelation . . . opened in those few pages." [6] Of all the essays in *Representative Men*, it alone develops a central hieroglyph. Apparently Emerson found it too difficult or inconvenient to construct a unique hieroglyph which would accommodate the biographical facts of the men he treats in each of the book's other lecture-essays. At times, however, imagery and particular remarks in these subsequent essays can be fully comprehended only in the light of "Uses of Great Men," the introductory essay. No doubt Emerson meant to give *Representative Men* some sort of general imagistic order, however vague, just as he would later use the hieroglyph of the One Man as a loose architectonic in *English Traits*.

The thesis of "Uses of Great Men" argues that personal individuality is merely an appearance, that great men actually represent mankind viewed collectively. Such individuals seem unique because the limits of human perspective prevent the average person from discerning the whole of which such individuals are a part. Their uniqueness, in fact, derives from an acuteness of vision which exceeds the insight of their contemporaries but which in reality signifies advancement eventually to be attained and surpassed by the human race. In this sense the great man serves as a spiritual guide to his time, a dynamic feature of his world, preventing men from wallowing forever in a morass of confusion caused by their present deficient insight.

Emerson emphasizes the image of sight throughout the essay. The great man opens "his eyes to see things in a true light" and in doing so he serves as "a collyrium to clear our eyes" (W, IV, 6, 25). The fact is, Emerson comments, "other men are lenses through which we read our own minds" (W, IV, 5); for "men have a pictorial or representative quality" (i.e., they are hieroglyphic) and "can paint, or make, or think, nothing but man" (W, IV, 8, 5). Emerson elevates this motif by noting that great men "satisfy expectation" (W, IV, 7), meaning that they provide a focus for the outward vision (*ex + spectare*) of others. Through them, as a picture or hieroglyph, people discover that "the mass of creatures and of qualities are still hid and expectant" (W, IV, 9). *Expectant* means, in this instance, not only awaiting discovery but also endowed with the latent capacity to mirror man's look. Typically Emerson suggests that subject and object are united through the act of human vision, an observation as true of man's relation to nature as it is of his relation to great men: "The possibility of interpretation lies in the identity of the observer with the observed" (W, IV, 11).

The preceding quotations, however, do not merely refer to Emerson's customary emphasis on sight. The image of vision contributes importantly to the central hieroglyph of the great man as explorer of the earth, particularly of an America-like New World. The vision of the great man discloses to others the "new possibilities" of life (W, IV, 32–33). His life and work become, in a sense, a report on a newly discovered region of vast yet hidden *expectations*. This report indicates, for instance, "how few materials are yet used by our arts" (W, IV, 9).

Emerson develops this motif in terms of imagery pertaining to wealth. The journal which is the life and work of the great man discloses that "the cheapness of man is every day's tragedy" and, consequently, it instructs us not to "think cheaply of ourselves, or of life" (W, IV, 31, 15). It promises profits and thereby "raises the credit of all the citizens" (W, IV, 4, 13). *Credit* implies faith (*credere*) in the value of one's expectations, and these expectations lie within as well as outside mankind. In short, the great man reveals the latent expectant wealth of the New World of the self.

Emerson broadens his wealth motif to include foodstuffs, appropriate in light of the value placed on such in the course of human exploration of the earth through the ages. Great men, it follows, "make the earth wholesome" and life on it "nutritious" (W, IV, 3). Their ideas provide "harvests for food" (W, IV, 7); others "feed on genius" (W, IV, 26). Through such harvests, as well as revelation of unmined value pertaining to the self, great men "enrich us" and generate "a new consciousness of wealth" (W, IV, 13, 18).

When Emerson remarks about the "vantage or purchase" (W, IV, 5) attained by our affection toward great men, he expands the context of and the reader's insight into the imagery of exploration and enrichment. *Purchase* refers to value obtained and also to an elevated point achieved by the exploration of the great man. The great man makes others wealthy in terms of heightened vision. From his own prominence he reveals life's "scale of degrees" which is informed by an "irresistible upward force" (W, IV, 20, 23). In relation to this scale and force "all things continually ascend" (W, IV, 11): "the chemic lump arrives at the plant, and grows; arrives at the quadruped, and walks; arrives at the man, and thinks" (W, IV, 11). This principle of ascent in nature becomes most manifest in the great man when the *expectation* of his explorer's eye meets and is mirrored by the expectancy of everything discovered in nature. Because he "inhabits a higher sphere of thought" as a consequence of this ascent, the great man—who in his role as representative is also the true artist—uses "the planet for his pedestal" (W, IV, 6, 7).

Emerson combines imagery of exploration and of ascent, with regard to his central hieroglyph of the sphere, through references to cartographic activity of the great man. Great men, Emerson writes, are "roadmakers" who reveal to others the way to "extend the area of life and multiply our relations" (W, IV, 13). The great man's life serves as a map "running out threads of relation through every thing"; by exploring life and subsequently disclosing wealth, he exemplifies "a rich and related existence" (W, IV, 9, 20). But maps are of limited use, Emerson warns; for "the best discovery the discoverer makes for himself" (W, IV, 28). Lest his readers should doubt that they all possess the spirit of the explorer evinced in the representative man, Emerson makes clear through the central hieroglyph that "each man is by secret linking connected with some district of nature, whose agent and interpreter he is" (W, IV,

9). The words *agent* and *interpreter* not only refer to man's role as an explorer reporting and serving as the link between man and his inner territory, but also specifically accentuate that facet of his exploration which activates nature upwardly into the region of thought. Man is the dynamic agent actualizing nature's expectancy: "Each material thing has its celestial side; has its *translation,* through humanity, into the spiritual and necessary sphere" (W, IV, 11; italics added).

From these remarks, particularly from the observation about the reflection of the subject in the object he explores and elevates, it is evident that cartographic activity of the great man ultimately produces a map of the human situation. As "the naturalist or geographer of the supersensible regions," he becomes "a definer and map-maker of the latitudes and longitudes of our condition" (W, IV, 16, 12–13). By mapping out man's rich relations or roadlike connections, the great man expands human horizons, a result suggested by Emerson through references to the encircling lines of longitude and latitude. In one instance Emerson says of the exploratory activity of the great man: "A new quality of mind travels by night and by day, in concentric circles from its origin" (W, IV, 33).[7]

The image of concentric circles implies expansion from within, which is precisely the principle evident in the "unfolding" education of the great man (W, IV, 8): "Man is that noble endogenous plant which grows, like the palm, from within outward" (W, IV, 6). When Emerson pronounces that "we are entitled to these enlargements" (W, IV, 17), he emphasizes by a play on words: (1) the idea of our internal expansion, which involves (2) the notion of our discovery of "new fields of activity" (W, IV, 16) and (3) the idea of our nobility (i.e., we are *titled,* a motif developed in the essay) in the light of (4) our legal ownership of these regions of possibility (i.e., we hold the title or deed).

The imaginary lines of longitude and latitude which the great man, as cartographer, draws around the human sphere derive from within himself—Emerson's word *meridian* (W, IV, 9) refers to latitudinal lines and to the highest points of human development as well. In contrast to most people who "take hold on the poles of the earth," the great man reaches upward and draws "his private ray unto the concave sphere" (W, IV, 12, 32). His cartographic lines of longitude and latitude are not restricted to the earth but expand outwardly from himself into the celestial dome, there to map the nature and condition of man; for, it should be recalled, he is "the naturalist or geographer of the supersensible regions." In his explorations he uses the world as a pedestal; and, as the Latin *ped* (foot) suggests, once we follow the lines of rich relations which the great man has mapped for us, we "shall never again be quite the miserable pedants we were" (W, IV, 17). To discover these roads of connections, however, requires an eye as discerning as that of the great man. "Some rays escape the common observer, and want a finely adapted eye" (W, IV, 32), Emerson notes, joking about the invisibility of the longitudinal and latitudinal lines. But they who can discern the longitude and latitude of the human condition, they who can map the "metre of the mind," themselves become hieroglyphic "metres or milestones of progress" (W, IV, 18, 34) for the collective humanity they pictorially represent.

In "Success"

In "Success" (1870) Emerson once more employs the image of the exploring cartographer as the governing hieroglyph. Although it presents some new and interesting features of the image, this hieroglyph functions less complexly than in the earlier essays discussed in this chapter. To some extent this simplicity may suggest Emerson's artistic decline; but if so, the evidence is moderate and discourages any attempt to dismiss his later writings as insignificant.

The motif of exploration in "Success" primarily utilizes imagery relating to Columbus and to America as the New World. Columbus, who "at Veragua found plenty of gold" (W, VII, 285), represents a model of the truly successful individual, one whose discoveries enrich others in the multiple sense attributed to the idea of wealth in "Uses of Great Men." But the explorer must also be a cartographer if his discovery is to profit others. Only by mapping his journey can he assure a return voyage, the point underlying Emerson's emphasis on Columbus's remark about his fellow seamen: "they can give no other account than that they went to lands where there was abundance of gold, but they do not know the way to return thither, but would be obliged to go on a voyage of discovery as much as if they had never been there before" (W, VII, 285). Columbus, Emerson concludes, "kept his private record of his homeward path" (W, VII, 285).

The key words in Emerson's observation about Columbus and the ideal he represents are *private, homeward,* and *path.* Throughout "Success," as in "Uses of Great Men," Emerson stresses the roadlike webs of relation resulting from the cartography of the great man. The word *path* belongs to this motif, which functions in terms of metaphors derived from the practical manifestations—Emerson, assuredly, is aware of the appropriateness of this source for his "New World" audience —of discoveries by the great man. The image of "lengthened lines of railroad and telegraph" (W, VII, 283) functions in the essay as the chief provenience of these metaphors for the far-reaching webs of relation engendered by Columbus-like discoveries.[8] Such lines of connection bring new wealth from the distant regions of man's world; they symbolize the wealth which awaits man in the realms beyond, yet related to the geophysical sphere. The genuine outcome of exploration does not lie in the tangible result seen in the railroad or the telegraph but in the spiritual fact they symbolize. "The world is enlarged for us," Emerson explains, "not by new objects, but by finding more affinities and potencies in those we have" (W, VII, 302; cf. Walt Whitman's "Passage to India" [1871]).

It is, of course, the self which roams the world, a traveling geologist or student of the earth, ever in expectation of discovery. Only the true lover, whose "eye and ear are telegraphs," possesses "finer sense than others" (W, VII, 303). He enjoys the capacity for "wide-seeing" or far vision, for the penetration of the illusion of phenomena, and for the perception of "the affirmative of affirmatives" (W, VII, 311, 309). This capacity, in regard to Emerson's hieroglyphic, explains why the explorer self—especially that of the American, who because of his Saxon lineage inherits the restlessness of Norsemen (W, VII, 287)—seeks to traverse the "enchanting waves" of life and, like Columbus and the creative artist, to announce, "behold a new world of dream-like glory" (W, VII, 300). The province of this explorer is to delineate the path or way, to convey "fine communications," manifesting the fact that "the world is always opulent" and fraught with the golden possibility of a new enriching discovery (W, VII, 306).

Emerson's remark about the privacy of Columbus's record is also important. The successful explorer, Emerson observes, has learned the value of self-reliance. He instinctively follows the advice of Michelangelo, who in his "course" as an artist explored new regions of perception: "to confide in one's self, and be something of worth and value" (W, VII, 291). The opulence of the New-World discovery lies, typically for Emerson, in the self and is thus realized through "self-possession" (W, VII, 295). The explorer telegraphs this self-worth to others from the vantage point (note Emerson's pun) of his inner discovery: "I gain my point, I gain all points, if I can reach my companion with any statement which teaches him his own worth" (W, VII, 294).

In delineating the path to and from the private self, Emerson intimates in his remark on Columbus's journal, the explorer extends the boundaries of what others define as home. To be more precise, he discloses that the new regions of his discovery have really always been a part of man's home, however unbeknownst to the owner. The "dulness of the multitude," in contrast to the far vision of the ideal explorer, prevents men from discerning "the house in the ground-plan" (W, VII, 293). This same lack of perception accounts for general ignorance of the possibility that "next door to you probably, on the other side of the partition in the same house, was a greater man than any you had seen" (W, VII, 305).

The greater man, like the true opulence he discovers, lies

within the unexplored area of the household of the inner self. The Columbus-like explorer merely gives expression to this greater man who dwells on the same sphere as we but who inhabits a different vantage point in the phenomenal world. By his interior discoveries he communicates to his neighbors the value of cherishing the "intellectual and moral sensibilities" and of wooing "them to stay and make their home with us" (W, VII, 301). The fact is that "the inner life sits at home," that "wherever any noble sentiment dwelt, it made the faces and house around to shine" (W, VII, 311, 296). The successful explorer extends the boundaries of home because he is "at home" within himself. This is what Emerson means—and note the pun on *home*—when he says of every discovery or advancement, "if you trace it home, you will find it rooted in a thought of some individual man" (W, VII, 297).

By discovering other rooms or points in the self, the ideal explorer remains youthful; each enriching discovery in the self "lives in the great present" and "makes the present great" (W, VII, 311). He is like the man whose "eyes opened as he grew older" and for whom "every spring was more beautiful to him than the last" (W, VII, 299). Like the child, for whom "the houses were in the air," he penetrates the limits of phenomena to the inner "tents of gold"—the opulent domicile which travels with the explorer—where dwells "the king he dreamed he was" (W, VII, 298).

The house motif in "Success" is not as complexly developed as that in "Politics" or "The Over-Soul." Nor is the essay on the whole as impressive as those with which it shares the central image of the traveling geologist or student-explorer of the earthly sphere; its hieroglyph flashes or glitters somewhat more dimly than do those of the earlier writings.

The essay does demonstrate how over the years Emerson modified features of a hieroglyph. In the progression from "Experience" and "Nature" through "Uses of Great Men" to "Success," one witnesses a simplification in Emerson's approach to and extension of the traveling-geologist (or geographer) and planetary-sphere hieroglyphs. This direction most likely testifies to Emerson's decline as an artist; it certainly indicates to some degree an exhaustion of old images and an impoverishment of imagination in creating new ones. It *may* also reveal Emerson's impatience, derived in part from a sense of having made his argument so many times before.

Yet, with all these observations granted, the simplicity of the central hieroglyph in "Uses of Great Men" and "Success," however indicative it might be of waning artistic talent, manages to appeal. In these two essays, particularly in the latter, Emerson may not have been his younger artistic self, but he was still admirably busy at his work.

IV

The Human Logos Hieroglyph

In "Self-Reliance"

In "Self-Reliance" (1841) Emerson introduces a hieroglyph based on the sun, which includes a traditional Christian pun, one particularly prominent in seventeenth-century poetry, on the Son of God or Logos. Although the sun represents the central source of light around which circle the other parts of the solar system, this arrangement, according to Emerson, accommodates subsequent creations of new, if similar, focal centers. The planets in turn, for instance, become smaller suns, attracting satellites and other smaller parts of creation. Moreover, commenting that "the genesis and maturation of a planet, its poise and orbit . . . are demonstrations of the self-sufficing and therefore self-relying soul" (W, II 70–71), Emerson emphasizes that the on-going creation of new focal centers includes the human soul. The "soul is light" (W, II, 66) and, like the sun in traditional Christian symbolism, signifies for Emerson the deity. Many Christian writers, of course, spoke in similar terms about the soul as a source of light, but generally they described this illumination as a passively reflected luminosity rather than as an actively self-initiated light of a miniature sun.[1] For Emerson, the soul is a sun because the deity it represents dwells within the individual. "What is deep is holy" because "the absolutely trustworthy" is "seated" in the heart (W, II, 73, 47).

Anticipating the accusation of critics schooled in more traditional Christian notions of the dependent will or heart, Emer-

son attempts to reverse the indictment by asserting that this
inner source of inspiration "cannot be denied without impiety
and atheism" (W, II, 64). This inner light is observable in the
great man, who serves as "the centre of things" and around
whom others "revolve by the gravitation of spirits" (W, II,
60, 70).

Emerson, as might be expected, stresses the ongoing creation of such inward centers of light and, in at least one notable
instance, he accentuates its importance in comparison to the
external sun: "A man should learn to detect and watch that
gleam of light which flashes across his mind *from within,* more
than the lustre of the firmament" (W, II, 45; italics added).
Nature's sun is, in Emerson's view, an emblem or picture of the
truth evident in the sunlike soul.

In "Self-Reliance" Emerson develops this hieroglyph and
makes further use of Christian tradition by associating the sun
with the concept of the Logos. The Logos or Word is the
sun/Son of God; he is the ever-dynamic divine agent who spoke
and continues to speak all things into being. As the Son of God,
he is the locus of the eternal transition between infinity and
finitude. Because Emerson sees the soul as a sun, he extends
the image to accommodate the idea that man, whose "power is
inborn" (W, II, 89), possesses a facility for genesis-like actions.
When he remarks, "to believe your own thought, to believe that
what is true for you in your private heart is true for all men,—
that is genius" (W, II, 45), he is referring to the inborn, absolutely trustworthy Logos-power deep in the self, a power which
complete individuals express as acts of creation or generation.
The words *genius, genesis,* and *genuine* suggest the Logos-like
self. Emerson believes that "genuine action will explain itself
and will explain . . . other genuine actions" (W, II, 59) because creative actions—genesis-like, hence genuine—performed
by the deity within the human self provide their own explanation. Like Yahweh, in response to Moses, all genuine acts assert, "I am what I am."

The circularity between subject (the deity in the self) and
object (the action) implied by this notion—an earlier version

(1841) of the pattern present in "Experience" (1844) and "Uses of Great Men" (1850)—defines the core of man's genuine acts of genesis. This idea of the union of creator and object is heretical viewed from older New England religious thought concerning an *ex nihilo* creation and a transcendent God— though generally speaking Puritan theology flirted with the notion of divine immanence in creation.[2] But the real focus of Emerson's heresy lies in his assertion that, in expressing the Logos-like dynamic between the divine inner self and the material action, "man is the word made flesh" (W, II, 76). This important remark, it is pertinent to note, does not appear in the original version of the passage in which it now occurs (EL, III, 265); Emerson carefully included it in the revised remark because it contributes crucially to the central hieroglyph of "Self-Reliance."

Enlarging the implications of this view of the inner Logos, Emerson observes that the great man will be a nonconformist even as was Jesus, traditionally thought to be the incarnation of God. Significantly Emerson reinforces this idea primarily in reference to the spoken word; according to Emerson, in every present act of independent speech man fulfills his Logos function. Of the Logos, he writes: "when God speaketh he should communicate, not one thing, but all things; should fill the world with his voice; should scatter forth light, nature, time, souls, from the centre of the present thought" (W, II, 65–66). Herein lies the significance of Emerson's advice earlier in the essay, "Speak what you think now in hard words and to-morrow speak what to-morrow thinks in hard words again" (W, II, 57). Like the traditional Logos, the self should continue at every present moment to speak truth into being. The expression derived from the inner Logos of each individual should "new date and new create the whole," just as the birth of the incarnate Son of God or Logos—traditionally depicted in Christian symbolism as a re-creation reasserting the spoken genesis detailed in the first book of the Bible—marked the end of an old order ("temples fall," Emerson notes) and the beginning of a new measurement of time (B.C. to A.D.): "Whenever a mind is simple and receives a divine wisdom, old things pass away. . . . All things are dissolved to their centre by their cause" (W, II, 66).

Echoing still another traditional Christian idea, the Logos' role in the act of creation as presented in the first book of the Bible, Emerson emphasizes the spontaneity of each present act of the Logos-like self. "The essence of genius [the Logos-like potentiality for genesis], of virtue [that which most fundamentally pertains to man, *vir*], and of life [being which exists because of genius and virtue] . . . we call Spontaneity or Instinct"; he adds, "We denote this primary wisdom as Intuition" (W, II, 64).

As evident in "The American Scholar," Emerson associates intuition (*in + tueri*, to look within) with seeing. In "Self-Reliance" he likewise accentuates this point. Perception is "as much a fact as the sun" (W, II, 65) because the light of truth or the insight one *intuits* emanates from the Logos-like self. Perception or intuition, it should be recalled, establishes the basis for expression: "all that we say is the far-off remembering of the intuition" (W, II, 68).

As in "The American Scholar," Emerson again associates intuition and its implication of sight with the feet. Insofar as civilized man is unable to tell the hour by the sun within him, he "has lost the use of his feet" (W, II, 85); such individuals should be invited to "take the shoes from off their feet, for God is here within" (W, II, 71). Typical of Emerson's artistry, this last remark contains a double entendre not only suggesting the intuitive proximity of the feet to the deity but also referring to a church which one should enter barefoot (this will be discussed further). Emerson's attention to intuition finally argues that in order to live in "the thousand-eyed present," man must strive to express the genius or creative capacity within him through the "new and spontaneous word" (W, II, 57, 54).

He realized, however, that most people fail to express their inner Godlike capacity. Most lack "the skill to tell the hour by the sun," which means that the average person does not live in the present of his inner sun, in the immediacy of "that gleam of light which flashes across his mind from within" (W, II, 85, 45). Ignorance of this inner sun and, it follows, of the inner divine Son-ship or Logos-feature of the self results in an impoverished condition in which "we but half express ourselves" (W, II, 46–47). The average individual does not speak the hard word of generation and consequently never gives expression to his internal divinity. Instead of circling the sunlike soul and generating a new creative present moment around which others might revolve, the average person tends to compute his "orbit" in relation to his past actions (W, II, 56).

The word *revolution*, referring to planetary orbits around the sun as well as to the Son of God's rebellion against an older Jewish order, allows Emerson to elaborate on his motif through imagery alluding to the American War of Independence as an example of a new focal center. In his scheme, this war signifies a new-dating expression of a re-creating revolution spoken forth by the Logos-like self of the American people; it yields a new center of illumination around which other nations revolve. The most specific correlation between the Biblical account of creation and the American revolution occurs in the third paragraph of "Self-Reliance," in a passage culled from an early lecture (EL, III, 139) because of its appropriateness. In this passage Emerson reminds his readers of their national heritage and destiny (as he does in other essays by specific references to the New-World image); they are not to be "cowards fleeing before a revolution, but guides, redeemers [like Jesus, whose Logos capacity abides in all men] and benefactors, obeying the Almighty effort and advancing on Chaos and the Dark" (W, II, 47). Throughout the essay references to the independent and rebellious mind join such allusions to Jesus with those to the American Revolution; both Jesus and the War of Independence represent expressions of the sun/Son principle in great people. For Emerson, in short, "a greater self-reliance must work a revolution in all the offices and relations of men" (W, II, 77).

Specifically this revolution (orbiting, rebellion) must occur within the hearts of individual Americans. Like the country as a whole, each American citizen must strive for self-sufficient independence, for freedom from "foreign taste" and "foreign support" (W, II, 82, 89). Emerson endorses a permanent revisionism in "Self-Reliance," as elsewhere, whenever he speaks of the necessity of continually abandoning the past for the revolutionary or creative present moment. "Let us enter into the state of war," Emerson proclaims, in imitation of the leaders of the War of Independence, whenever a rebellion will enable us to perform what is right; and, he puns, "the only right is what is after [our] constitution" (W, II, 72, 50). The essence of the self, like that of a country, is reflected in the laws of its constitution. The legal aspect of Emerson's play on the word *constitution* reverberates throughout "Self-Reliance." The essay is replete with references to trials, to sentences, to being committed or jailed (to be committed to past causes is to be sentenced to imprisonment), to conspiracies (paradoxically "society everywhere is in conspiracy against the manhood [virtue] of every one of its members" [W, II, 49]), to showing cause, to secondary testimony, to paying fines, and to being whipped. One must be ever ready to wage war if he is to "obey no law less than the eternal law" (W, II, 73), which law is the principle of revolution asserting one's alignment to his own constitution.

For Emerson, the Latin roots *con* and *sto* suggest that the law of the human *constitution* dictates that man should stand up. This is, as we saw, the pictorial message of "The American Scholar" and "Politics." In "Self-Reliance," to be creative or revolutionary is to stand erect, as Emerson intimates by observing that "when private men shall act with original views, the lustre will be transferred from the actions of kings to those of gentlemen" (W, II, 63). In other words, the private or independent individual acts or exercises the transforming power of his will whenever he sees creatively or originally; the word *original,* for Emerson, plays on the meaning of its Latin source, *oriri* (to rise). Originality, then, refers to the act of rising up in one's self; in terms of the related political terminology so prevalent in the essay, it signifies an internal uprising or revolution.

In the same passage in which he speaks of the original action of the private man, Emerson also refers to the result of an internal uprising: the transference of kingly dignity to the actions of gentlemen. Significantly this comment suggests that an internal revolution will, like the American War of Independence, bestow upon each individual the dignity previously reserved for a monarch. Realization of this facet of the American dream lies within the self. If one should indeed "rise up," if he should truly possess *original* vision and satisfy the law of his constitution, he would discover that his "rejected thoughts" no longer "come back to [him] with a certain alienated majesty" (W, II, 45–46); for he then awakens, "exercises his reason and finds himself a true prince" (W, II, 62)—an image which, as we have discussed, Emerson would use again in "Politics." When man realizes this princeliness derived from his internal divinity (sun/Son), he will no longer be mendicant: "as soon as the man is at one with God, he will not beg," Emerson writes, for having discovered worth in himself that person cannot feel poor (W, II, 77). He discovers within the self the real New World, a place of "native riches" and of "living property" which "perpetually renews itself" (W, II, 71, 88). The region of the self, in other words, is infinite and so are its as yet undiscovered riches.

This process of successive yet never ending disclosures of wealth defines the principle of revolution Emerson advocates, the principle of turning around the sun of the self and of giving expression to the ever-new creating Logos of the self around which others will temporarily circle. In this way society is *improved,* Emerson's word meaning "turned to profit." Hence individuals become wealthy princes, and the ultimate profit of social improvement is "the triumph of *principles*" (W, II, 90; italics added to indicate the nuance). Like Jesus, every man is the word made flesh, the revolutionary sun/Son around whom others revolve, the Prince of princes. In this context Emerson concludes that "mutual reverence . . . is due from man to man" (W, II, 63).

In one place in the essay Emerson remarks that until man realizes that he is a prince, palaces will convey to him "an alien and forbidding air" (W, II, 62). This comment, pertaining to the notion that man should become the lord of his household, provides a transition point for including a house motif; the primary word he uses in relation to it is *institution*. In this earlier version of the motif, also to be used in "Politics," institution refers to anything of the past so established that it imprisons the present (note Emerson's dovetailing of legal imagery relating to the constitution motif). The word refers, as well, to something that stands (*in + statuere*). Like *original* and *constitution, institution* refers to man's capacity for standing. All institutions evolve from this capacity and, mirrorlike, remind men of it: "an institution is the lengthened shadow of one man" (W, II, 61). Institutions are the erections constructed around the revolutionary and original action of one person— the emergence of Christianity from Jesus, for instance.

As such, institutions are excellent, but they should not become ossified structures imprisoning the present creative act any more than the person from whom it derives should remain a permanent center of attraction. There is, Emerson writes, "a united light on the advancing actor" (W, II, 59) which casts further shadows from other great men; which is to say, institutions should readily give rise to still other institutions. Precisely this point—never, to my knowledge, recognized by those who cite the passage—informs Emerson's assertion that "a foolish consistency is the hobgoblin of little minds" (W, II, 57). *Consistency*, like *constitution*, means to stand (*com + sistere*); standing is important for Emerson, but a foolish stance is undesirable.

In view of the Biblical and theological imagery associated with the central hieroglyph of the sun, including its religious reference to the Son of God, it is not surprising that the church is the *institution* most frequently mentioned in "Self-Reliance." This emphasis is appropriate in light of Emerson's assessment in the essay of the atheism of the established church. The church motif, somewhat different from that in "The Over-Soul," provides a nodal point around which several images cluster. Emerson claims, for example, that the preacher who pretends to examine "the grounds of the institution" which is his church really functions as "a retained attorney" (W, II, 54–55) working in the service of a foolish consistency imprisoning constitutional rights. He contributes, in Emerson's opinion, to "the vain [foolish/futile] end" for which so many meeting houses "now *stand*" (W, II, 52; italics added). The true church lies within the human self—Emerson equates windows to eyes and the doorway to the mouth in the essay—and in this self man, though at present his "housekeeping is mendicant" (W, II, 75), will discover the princely divinity or Logos capacity he possesses.

Giving rise to one's own inner church or institution, derived from the divinity of the self, will be impeded as long as "the luminaries of heaven seem . . . hung on the arch their master built" (W, II, 80; Emerson specifically added the image of the arch to the original version of this remark [JMN, VII, 28; EL, III, 141]). Man must strive to see beyond the limitations of the confining church structure or institution, to "perceive that light, unsystematic, indomitable, will break into any cabin" (W, II, 80). This vision depends on the discovery that the true ground or foundation of an institution lies in the intuition informing the great man, whose spontaneous creative actions engendered it as a shadow of himself. Thus out of reverence, one must walk barefoot (recall Emerson's association of feet with instinct) in the church of the self in order to maintain contact with this ground of intuition; it is in the inexplicable "deep force" of the holy self that "all things find their common origin" or source of rising (W, II, 64). As a result of this ground of intuition, which is transformed through human action into thought, the walls of these very institutions "will crack, will lean, will rot and vanish, and the immortal light, all young and joyful, million-orbed, million-colored, will beam over the universe as on the first morning" (W, II, 80). This light is indeed "indomi-

table"—uncontainable (*domitare*) and un-dome-able (*domus,*
house); and with each successive revolutionary re-creation or
first morning "temples fall" (W, II, 66), even as they did from
the revolution represented by the advent of Christianity. In
"Self-Reliance" Emerson presents his ideas as another revolutionary advancement, one before which the current institution
of the Christian church will fall.

This process of raising and leveling institutions pinpoints
precisely the dynamic expression of the Logos in the self.
Through the activating force of the self, the will—that transition between the ground of instinct and the conscious erection
of institutions—man becomes the word made flesh. He mediates eternally between what is and what will be; by eternally
transforming instinct into conscious reality, he mediates between the divine in the self and the material in the world.
Through this dynamic of mediation, in the midst of the endless revolution or re-creation he continually initiates, man paradoxically attains stability: "In the Will work and acquire, and
thou hast chained the wheel of Chance, and shall sit thereafter
out of [free of] fear from her rotations" (W, II, 89).

The image of sitting is important in this remark as it is
throughout "Self-Reliance." Recall, for instance, the statement
that the absolutely trustworthy is seated in the heart (W, II,
47); Emerson deleted the word *stirring* from the first two versions (JMN, VII, 12; EL, III, 139) and carefully substituted
the word *seated*. Together with kneeling (W, II, 77–78), sitting serves as an image for the will, as the potential active
power uniting instinct (feet) and consciousness (standing)—
hand imagery dramatizing action of the will also abounds in
the essay and is discussed later. The wise man who "stays at
home" sits relaxed amidst revolutions (W, II, 81). Sitting depicts a balanced posture of transition between pre-revolutionary
impulse and post-revolutionary institutionalization, between
primeval chaos (imaged in the essay in terms of mobs) and
extended shadows of rationality and order. Sitting and kneeling
symbolize the will, that mysterious inner power in the self
which "ceases in the instant of repose; it resides in the moment

of transition from the past to a new state" (W, II, 69; the image of repose does not appear in the original version of this remark [JMN, VII, 518]). "So let us always sit," Emerson urges his audience, emphasizing *always* as well as *sit; "*let us sit at home with the cause" (W, II, 71). Such sitting becomes possible when one recognizes that the church or palace or home which lies within him encompasses more than does any external institution, however organic the latter may be to the former. Only when one achieves this paradoxically relaxed or calm state of dynamic interaction between unconscious instinct and conscious rationality can he, Logos-like, give creative external expression to "the sense of being which in *calm* hours *rises,* we know not how, in the soul" (W, II, 64; italics added).

Varying the concluding portrait of "The American Scholar," "Self-Reliance" dramatically illustrates the image of sitting. In the later essay Emerson makes clearer that standing or forming *institutions* represents man's *constitution* less than the fact of his capacity for *originality,* for the process of giving rise to things. The person who realizes and actualizes his human destiny "throws himself unhesitatingly on his thought, instantly rights himself, stands in the erect position, commands his limbs, works miracles" (W, II, 89). Ideally—and in an image considerably more benign than that of man's rise and fall in "Experience" would be—the process is endless: institutions give way to revolutionary impulses, which in turn engender new institutions, and other sunlike forces, other Sons of God, perform miracles surpassing earlier ones. In this manner, Emerson argues, the actor—the ever-speaking and ever-creating Logos, the word made flesh—advances as the light he expresses increasingly brightens.

In "Worship"

As the preceding remarks indicate, Emerson used both a central hieroglyph (the sun) and its related idea (the Son of God) to realize an underlying order in "Self-Reliance." In "Worship" (1860) he employs another feature of the Logos concept as the nucleus of his imagery and motifs: the prophet mediating between the eternal and the mundane. Strictly speaking, "Worship," like many other essays in *The Conduct of Life,* does not have a central visual image of quite the pictorial sense this book has defined. Its use of the Logos-function of the prophet, however, does operate rather similarly to a hieroglyph and illustrates once again how in later essays Emerson both simplified and yet developed aspects of a unifying system of imagery previously employed.

Emerson begins the essay by identifying himself with the prophet's role: "I am sure that a certain truth will be said through me, though I should be dumb, or though I should try to say the reverse" (W, VI, 201). Through the Logos-function of the word, spoken (principally) or silent, "the kingdom of the senses and the understanding" is joined to "that of ideas and imagination" (W, VI, 224). For him, the true prophets, those "appointed by God Almighty," are "souls out of time, extraordinary, prophetic . . . who are rather related to the system of the world than to their particular age and locality" (W, VI, 212, 205). Emerson understands the function of prophets in the Old Testament sense; they do not predict the future, but rather they are preaching men of action who believe themselves to be the mouthpieces of Yahweh and the instruments of His creative design. As the essay advances, with references to Isaiah and Jeremiah as well as to an anecdote about a false prophet (W, VI, 203, 227–28), Emerson indicates that, although certain individuals "are nearer to the secret of God than others" (W, VI, 217), everyone latently possesses the gift of prophecy in some form. This idea informs his account of the Shaker belief that "the Spirit will presently manifest to the man himself and to the society what manner of person he is, and whether he belongs among them" (W, VI, 237). One should, in Emerson's opinion, imitate Benedict's assessment of himself as a servant of the Spirit (W, VI, 235), as a prophet mediating between divine influences and mundane reality.

Emerson makes use of the traditional Christian concept of the indwelling Spirit—"God builds his temple in the heart" (W, VI, 204)—to explain the Logos-like prophetic nature of man: "There is a principle which is the basis of things, which all speech aims to say, and all action to evolve, a simple, quiet, undescribed, undescribable presence, dwelling very peacefully in us, our rightful lord" (W, VI, 213). This divine principle, this spiritual force, animates man and gives him what is generally thought of as a soul (*anima*). The Spirit is "the dim dictator behind" all individuals, who are its prophetic subjects "with their will or against their will" (W, VI, 228–29); it is, typically for Emerson, the same principle that "tyrannizes at the centre of nature" (W, VI, 202). The soul in man and the Over-Soul in the universe share this Spirit or principle of animation. God "delegat[es] his divinity to every particle," Emerson explains; "man is made of the same atoms as the world is, he shares the same impressions, predispositions and destiny" (W, VI, 221–22, 240).

The soul or principle of animation is, for Emerson, most evident in the human will. That the will remains central in the work of the Spirit is a traditional Christian notion, perhaps receiving particular emphasis in Puritan dogma. In order to fulfill his prophetic function, one must first, according to Emerson, be a passive recipient: "we are not to do, but to let do; not to work, but to be worked upon" (W, VI, 213). In Emerson's scheme the spontaneous impulse or instinct informs the will and, like grace in Puritan theology, empowers it to act; the will is not a faculty but the very moment of transition between instinct and thought.

To fulfill his Logos-like prophetic function each person must strive for the animation of the mediating will and thereby participate in the upward flow from form to spirit. As the word made flesh, man serves the Spirit as the medium for this endless transformation "of the inflexible law of matter into the subtile kingdom of will and of thought" (W, VI, 219). Everyone performs this act of mediation with his will or against his will; but the true prophet, the great man, actively embraces the passivity of his role as the Spirit's servant. This idea of active passivity—its Hegelian implications notwithstanding— derives in part from Emerson's New England Puritan heritage [3] just as do so many other features of his emphasis on the will in "Worship," including his use of the conventional phrases "a voluntary obedience, a necessitated freedom" (W, VI, 240) to indicate further the nature of this disposition (the phrases also suggest the darker cast of Emerson's later thought). Through the Augustinian virtues of love, humility, and faith (W, VI, 231), Emerson explains, one can exercise his actively passive will with the prophetic "conviction that his work is dear to God" (W, VI, 232). Through the prophet's will "the whole revelation . . . is vouchsafed" (W, VI, 238).

Throughout "Worship" Emerson again uses hand imagery to dramatize the action of the will. Interestingly, however, the hand imagery in this work particularly recalls the traditional Christian motifs of swords, combat, and victories. The acts of hands represent in the essay both modes of the will's expression: deeds and words (W, VI, 213). Actions, whether deeds or words, constitute man's prophetic duty. In "The Poet" Emerson stressed this same point, "Words are also actions, and actions are a kind of words" (W, III, 8), an idea equally evident in the concept of the Logos as the *spoken* word or, synonymously, as the *act* of creation. The prophet's deeds are principally verbal, as Emerson indicates in his initial identification with the role of the Spirit's servant. His function, as an intermediary between the divine and the mundane, is to "announce absolute truth" (W, VII, 205).

Because he believes words are deeds, Emerson readily associates prophetic action with images of construction, particularly the creation of a church (as in "Self-Reliance" and, in a different but related way, in "The Over-Soul"). According to Christian tradition, God is "the builder of heaven" as well as the fashioner of "his temple in the heart" (W, VI, 204) through the Logos. But, as we have noted, in Emerson's scheme man bears this Logos function within himself; he is the word made flesh. Consequently prophetic man serves as an agent through whom the divine architect achieves this construction, most perfectly through the voluntary obedience or the active passivity of the former's will (i.e., proper action). The Spirit's servant, then, should avoid deference to lower (*sub*-urban) trends symbolized by the cheap houses manifest in "the suburban fashion in building" (W, VI, 223). The principle of ascent informs a true construction, as Emerson indicates in his use of an image of successive ruins to suggest a rising foundation: "God builds his temple in the heart on the ruins of churches and religions" (W, VI, 204). Since, as Emerson remarks, genuine prophets transcend "their particular age and locality," they are not attracted to the proximity of suburban constructions but rather turn to the ever-indomitable (un-dome-able) and distant "new Church" which has "heaven and earth for its beams and rafters" (W, VI, 241). The design perceived in nature delineates precisely that intended for the heart; both are built by God and both, in sharing the same atoms endowed with their Creator's divinity, receive "the same impressions, predispositions and destiny" (W, VI, 240). Through the transforming Logos-like prophetic power of his will, man serves as the Spirit's deputized architect for this inner and outer church: "When his mind is illuminated, when his heart is kind, he throws himself joyfully [the image of willed action is deliberate] into the sublime order, and does, with knowledge, what the stones do by structure" (W, VI, 240). Such genuine actions (words and deeds) of the prophet-architect make others "think they walk in hallowed cathedrals" (W, VI, 231).[4]

Emerson, in the later phase of his career reflected in "Worship," realizes more than ever before the difficulty the prophet faces in trying to erect his church. This person is liable to be misunderstood and disregarded, even as were the Old Testament prophets. Moreover, there is, Emerson admits, a fixed law of necessity. Yet, paradoxically, that very law yields confidence to man, for it points to the inevitability of evolutionary (Emerson's word) ascent.[5]

Like George Herbert, Emerson relishes the positive aspect of predestination, the fact that luck is nonexistent because "the dice are loaded" (W, VII, 221). If man possesses character, he accepts the "necessitated freedom" of his condition and through voluntary obedience acts in compliance with the universal scheme reflected in nature and in the human heart. In this way "we are the builders of our fortunes" (W, VI, 221), of our luck or fate (*fortuna*) because we are architects of the true church. This new construction, always grounded on the increasingly elevated foundation of the ruins of a previous system, ascends or progresses upwardly.

Like Isaiah and Jeremiah, whom he specifies in the essay, Emerson announces the destruction of the present Jerusalem which shall give rise to a new one. This is a period of transition, he explains, a time of joy not of despair. The apparent current "anarchy in our ecclesiastic realms" really betokens a new beginning, founded on the ruins of a previous order, akin to that represented by the chaos of the American Revolutionary War or evinced on the frontier "slope of the Rocky Mountains or Pike's Peak" (W, VI, 204).[6] Emerson encourages his readers to join their work to his words, together to exercise fully man's prophetic role. "To make our *word* or *act* sublime," he writes, "we must make it real" (W, VI, 226; italics added). Emerson means that man must make it spiritual; indeed, he explains, "the true meaning of *spiritual* is *real*" (W, VI, 215). This process of spiritualization implies ascent and refers specifically to the endless elevating action of the Logos-like will transforming impulse into thought.

Emerson indicates in the final paragraph of "Worship" that man "needs only his own verdict" (W, VI, 241) when he properly exercises his will in prophetic words and deeds. A *verdict* is a judgment, and the word nicely implies his view of human self-reliance derived from a confidence in the spoken word or the performed action as expressions of the Spirit. Such words and deeds pass judgment on themselves because there exists no higher authority than the Spirit from which they derive. *Verdict* also suggests the Latin meaning of the word (*versus* + *dictum*), to speak the truth. Because man's words and deeds prophetically articulate the truth, they circularly pass judgment on themselves. Whenever, in this double sense, man finds his own verdict self-sufficient, he realizes his latent vocation as soothsayer or mediating Logos-like prophet of truth and reality.

In "Farming"

One of Emerson's minor essays, "Farming" (1870), deserves a few words because its internal structure is derived from another aspect of the Logos-like self: the priestly role of the farmer. This central idea is not as completely developed as are the Son of God and prophet motifs in "Self-Reliance" and "Worship." Doubtless the hieroglyphic system to which it belongs had become redundant for Emerson by the time of the publication of *Society and Solitude*. Whereas in "Worship" Emerson focuses on the prophetic aspect of the self mediating between Spirit and matter, in "Farming" he stresses the priestly function of intermediating between matter and Spirit. Emerson does not, finally, emphasize a clear distinction between these two roles because, as in the example of Christ, one implies the other in his system.

As a "minister" (W, VII, 138, 153), the farmer serves as an administrator and "representative of Nature" (W, VII, 153). This observation means, for Emerson, that the farmer stands "nearest to God" (W, VII, 137). Upon his priestly powers— Emerson's notion of priesthood includes primitive ideas as well as contemporary ones—depend health, wealth, and marriage (W, VII, 140). The farmer-priest reveals the divine element underlying the apparent reality of phenomena, "the power that lurks in petty things" (W, II, 146). The activity of farming, stimulated by this power within the ministerial farmer, reveals the same divine force in nature; it indicates the fluid principle of expansion beneath the apparent solidity of matter. To utilize "sacred power" (W, II, 144) in this manner is the farmer's ministerial duty; through the activity of his hands in farming— that is, through the action of his will—he takes "the gas we have hoarded, mingle[s] it with water, and let[s] it be free to grow in plants and animals and obey the thought of man" (W, VII, 144).

Thought is the product of the intellect, and the "intellect is a fire" (W, VII, 145);[7] through the "fire of thought" solidity gives way to fluid reality, even as "air is matter subdued by heat" and provides "the receptacle from which all things spring, and into which they all return" (W, VII, 144–45). In the natural scheme of things, "the invisible and creeping air takes form and solid mass"; even "huge mountain chains are made up of gases and rolling wind" (W, VII, 144–45; cf. "Rubies" [1867], W, IX, 217).

This fact that "all things are flowing" is revealed through the exercise of the farmer's will in agricultural activity, through his mediating or priestly role yoking natural fact and divine thought (W, VII, 145). Hieroglyphically representing all mankind, the ministerial farmer "changes the face of the landscape" (W, VII, 153).

In this sense "the farmer is the *minder*" (W, VII, 142). His work depicts the transformational power of the human mind (instinct, will, and thought). But the word *minder* also refers to the idea that in expressing the power of thought the farmer fulfills man's Adamic role (W, VII, 153) of minding, administering, or looking after creation. As a "representative of Nature" close to the divine source, as in fact the very crown of creation, man is a priest mediating between the world below him in the scale of being and the spiritual realm toward which he and all under his charge are slowly ascending.

Emerson suggests that Man's charge is to administer "the great household of Nature" (W, VII, 140). Throughout "Farming," however, he develops this image in reference to the "great factory of our Copernican globe" (W, VII, 142). This remark, representing a variation of house and church motifs in many earlier essays, coalesces seemingly conflicting imagery in such a manner that the essay's hieroglyph reveals a covert feature of its symbolic significance. Not only is "every plant . . . a manufacturer of soil," but the entire "earth is a machine which yields almost gratuitous service to every application of intellect" (W, VII, 144). Man should look after or mind this factory by putting it to use through the application of moral and intellectual power; without this power it cannot function. A factory is a place for working, a place where the hand (will) is most crucial. This implied stress on the activity of working and especially on the use of hands makes the factory motif a perfect correlative for the image of the farmer's manual labors. Through these labors, through the transforming ministerial power of the human will, natural fact is manufactured into thought, just as in "The American Scholar" a "mulberry leaf is converted into satin" (CW, I, 59).

Motifs pertaining to the farmer as administrator of nature's factory similarly coalesce in Emerson's reference to "a basement story more valuable and that promises to pay a better rent than all the superstructure" (W, VII, 150). The administrator discovers in the cellar or power room of nature's factory exactly what the farmer discloses in his ministry of the earth, that beneath and infusing everything lies the sacred force of spontaneous impulse. The farmer favors such lowlands because they are made rich by the successive dissolution of previous forms (ideas), which endlessly provide a rich substance for new growth; in the "lowlands" the "wash of mountains has accumulated the best soil" (W, VII, 152).

Through exercise of the priestly role of his mediating will, man exerts sacred "powers and utilities" (W, VII, 153) to direct creation upward toward its divine source, that same source paradoxically evident in the subterranean impulse informing human action. Man, as the son of Adam, dwells close to that source. As Emerson's hieroglyph of the priestly farmer intends subtly to convey, man's duty is to realize the ministerial capacities of his self and to exercise them by administering nature's factory.

In "The Poet"

"The Poet" (1844) has justifiably played a significant part in commentaries on Emerson's aesthetic notions. Strangely its own aesthetic features have gone undetected, an irony compounded by the fact that the essay represents a masterful and unique achievement in Emerson's artistry. "The Poet" does not develop around the idea of the Logos as we have so far defined it, but has the mythological figure of Pan as its governing hieroglyph. Because he is half animal and half man, Pan symbolizes for Emerson a mediating position akin to that of the Logos-like self defined in "Self-Reliance" and suggested by the prophetic and priestly functions in "Worship" and "Farming." In "The Poet" Emerson was rather sensitive to Pan's adverse reputation, which taken at face value would have made the god a particularly inappropriate source for a hieroglyph. Always on the alert for the truth beneath surface deceptions, Emerson was certain, as he would remark in "Nature," that "frivolity is a most unfit tribute to Pan, who ought to be represented in the mythology as the most continent of gods" (W, III, 177). In June 1836 he had written in his journal: "I love the wood god. I love the mighty PAN" (JMN, V, 179).[8]

Using Pan as a hieroglyph must have appealed to Emerson on several levels. It would allow him to make use of a fable; in his opinion fables are like proverbs and allegories because they embody intuitive folk expressions of universal truths. Moreover, as he would have to "rectify" the mistaken impression of the meaning of the Pan myth, the fable would also permit him to exercise his penchant for the unconventional. The latter aim must have touched on still a third likely attraction, the opportunity to indicate the intuitive wisdom of the fable by creatively using the image of Pan as a viable emblem. In this regard it is pertinent, I think, that Emerson remarks in the essay how "we are far from having exhausted the significance of the few symbols we use" (W, III, 18). The significance of an emblem drawn from any fable lies in its signmaking (*signum + facere*) value, in its ability to serve throughout time as an exponent of new thought. Signs, symbols, emblems are universal; "nature offers all her creatures to [man] as a picture-language," Emerson reiterates, and "men of every class" are driven "to the use of emblems" (W, III, 13, 16). This belief in the universal appeal of the picture to man informs Emerson's aesthetic use of the hieroglyph in his essays.

In the figure of Pan, Emerson sees an emblem of the union of animal instinct and human consciousness, particularly in the fact that its human head—and the beautiful music it produces —is supported by sensuous goat legs. The underlying image

Emerson has in mind is established in an apparent generalization that "the beautiful rests on the foundations of the necessary" (W, III, 13). Most men, in Emerson's opinion, yield only to the level of sense (feet) and fail to transform this animal receptivity into the beauty of expressed thought (head). Most people, in other words, utilize but half of their Panlike nature: "The man is only half himself, the other half is his expression" (W, III, 5). In fact, however, "within the form of every creature is a force impelling it to ascend into a higher form" (W, III, 20).

The poet represents man in the fulness of his Panlike nature, for he knows how "to receive and to impart" (W, III, 6). Because he joins the two extremities of his being (feet/sense and head/beauty), the poet sees, handles, and speaks (W, III, 6)—activities, it should be recalled, corresponding to intuition (feet), will (hands), and intellect (head) respectively. "The poet is the person in whom these powers are in balance" (W, III, 6) because the ceaseless activity of his will brings about a dynamic equilibrium between the extremities of his nature. He accepts the animal portion of his self as crucial to his higher mental capacities. He knows that "in every word he speaks," he "rides" on sensations "as the horses of thought" (W, III, 21).[9] Similarly resorting to horse imagery as a correlative for the goat legs of the Panlike self, Emerson remarks about an important lesson the poet teaches: just "as the traveller who has lost his way throws his reins on his horse's neck and trusts to the instinct of the animal to find his road, so must we do with the divine animal who carries us through this world" (W, III, 27).

Most people, Emerson indicates, receive a new thought, a "new and higher fact" (W, III, 21), at the level of sensation but fail to transform it into still another more advanced thought. Instead of treating the innovative idea merely as new ground for further thought, they try to make it permanent and consequently prevent the lower animal impulse from dynamically metamorphosing into a high intellectual achievement. When people try to perpetuate an idea, Emerson suggests, they strive to live only in terms of the lower half of their being, the animal level of receptivity. To assert a belief in some idea as if it had the permanence of absolute truth is equivalent to living an animal life of pure sensation, one which ignores the upper expressive human feature of the Panlike self. Paradoxically such sensuous living impedes his sensitivity to the very instinct, to the "rays or appulses" which "arrive at the senses" (W, III, 6), that this lower region of man can detect. Such impulses, however, operate smoothly and beneficently only when the entire dynamic between sensation (feet) and thought (head) is uninhibited.

Thus, just as by means of his words the poet rides on sensations "as the horses of thought," so too should those very words become sensations or horses of further thought for his audience: "all language is vehicular and transitive, and is good, as ferries and horses are" (W, III, 34).

This comment pertains as well to Emerson's practice of his own art. The hieroglyph and all related motifs in an essay demonstrate use of conventional imagery (the myth of Pan, for example) in a new manner without dominating the focus of reader attention; rather, since every symbol is fugitive (W, III, 20), it should convey in a subliminal fashion an impulse to the reader's inner eye, stimulating it into the production of still another insight.

In contrast, when language, like the ideas it communicates, is treated as permanent, it loses its vehicular or horselike quality. This is the point of a comment Emerson paraphrases from Swedenborg: "Certain priests, whom he describes as conversing very learnedly together, appeared to the children who were at some distance, like dead horses" (W, III, 36). Masterful and poetically suggestive, this sentence indicates that the language and ideas (learned discourse) which gave rise to an institution (of which the priests are caretakers), because of their institutionalization, are no longer capable of conveying new thought (hence the image of dead horses); this fact appropriately is sensed by a new generation (children who are closer to the impulse because of their youth). Finally, the point about the

learnedness of the priests' conversation is ironic; for the un-
schooled children see more from their distant perspective than
do the wardens of institutionalized wisdom.

When the extremities of the Panlike self, when sensation
(feet) and thought (head) interact (hands/will) harmoni-
ously, one is enabled to express himself; he receives *and* imparts. The poet, Emerson's representative of this ideal man, is
like Pan in that, as a result of his internal harmony, he creates
music. He penetrates the "noise" of life to "that region where
the air is music," where one hears "primal warblings" (W, III,
12, 8).

This bird image provides an appropriate ancillary emblem
because, like that of Pan, it reinforces Emerson's belief about
the fundamental interaction between the lower and the upper
regions of the self. Like Pan, most birds (one of nature's symbols) live in two realms: the ground and the sky. Throughout
the essay Emerson coalesces music and bird imagery in order
to suggest the melodious flight toward which the upper region
of man aspires. Thus he speaks of men's proneness to permit
the lower half of their nature to dominate as a condition in
which they "hear, through all the varied music, the *ground-
tone* of conventional life" (W, III, 9; italics added). Although
man shall never permanently inhabit "the all-piercing, all-
feeding and ocular air of heaven" (W, III, 12) any more than
can a bird, he is not permanently grounded. He can delight in
the possibility of flight, particularly as demonstrated by the
poet, the "winged man, who will carry [him] into the heaven"
(W, III, 12) in flights of birdlike song.

Revealing the darker side of his thinking, Emerson comments that most often the poet "does not know the way into the
heavens, and is merely bent that [someone] should admire his
skill to rise like a fowl or a flying fish, a little way from the
ground or the water" (W, III, 12). The word *bent* does not
solely refer to the poet's inclination (*O.E.D.*, p. 806) but also
indicates the predestined shape of his disposition. He is bent in
the sense that, like Pan, he can never stand erect. In the dynamic of its activity, his Panlike nature is suspended between

crawling like an animal on the earth and standing fully erect like a man with a perfect physique. This is a clever variation of Emerson's use of images of muscular activity in "Experience," of man's effort to balance himself on a ball in "Nature," and, in an earlier, more serene version, of man's relaxed sitting in "Self-Reliance." The poet is stooped or bent by his very nature, and, as with the bird, his flight is merely an arc rising from the earth's curved surface only to return to that ground once again.

Nevertheless, and here is the optimistic note, the dynamics of this flight between the ground of sensation and the realm of celestial thought, the exercise of the power that comprises the will, provides the source of human dignity and engenders beauty. Even though the beauty "which *flies* before him" is but "half seen," yet "by and by he says something which is *original* and *beautiful*" (W, III, 39; italics added). What the poet says rises up (*oriri*/original) and flies (beauty flies, Emerson writes) like a bird.[10] "Clad with wings (such was the virtue of the soul out of which they came)," his songs or poems ascend above "the solid *ground* of historical evidence" and "leap and pierce into the deeps of infinite time" (W, III, 23, 4, 24; italics added). Mankind gains something tangible from this poetic expression, for with each subsequent landing the ground changes. Genuine flights do not permit man to "tumble down again soon into [his] old nooks" but, on the contrary, reveal "another world, or nest of worlds" (W, III, 12–13, 30).

Emerson's references, in two passages already discussed, to flying fish and the deeps of infinite time alert the reader to another motif in the essay. For Emerson, as for Thoreau in *Walden,* the infinitude of the celestial sphere corresponds to the depths of the self, the waters of which are "so deep, that we hover [note the bird image] over them with a religious regard" (W, III, 15). To plummet the depths of the self is to soar into the heavens in song; for both the upper region (human head/expression) and the lower region (animal legs/sensation) participate in a single dynamic. The sea provides a mirror image of the sky; and man descends into the self in order to ascend into the celestial realm of beauty, as Emerson indicates in the following remark suggesting the constellations of the zodiac: "the great deep is adorned with animals, with men, and gods" (W, III, 21). That heavenly beauty lies within the depths of the self, that up is down and down is up, is consummately depicted in Emerson's paradoxical observation that man is "a heavenly tree, growing with his root, which is his head, upward" (W, III, 31).

Because the poet is the individual in whom the lower and upper features of man's Panlike nature operate in dynamic balance, his song combines the two extremes. Since his song flies like beauty (W, III, 23, 39), it must by poetic substitution be beautiful. Beauty, Emerson observes in the last paragraph of "The Poet," can be witnessed "wherever day and night meet in twilight" (W, III, 42). Appropriately, the poet's song joins the light of day and the darkness of night in the sense that it represents the dynamic interaction between sensation, which is depicted throughout the essay in images of darkness and opacity (the deeps), and thought, which is portrayed throughout in images of morning light and transparency (the heavens). Mounting above the "clouds and opaque airs" of life existing at the level of form or sensation (including, of course, the opacity of institutionalized ideas), the *genuine* poem reveals "forms with transparent boundaries" (a phrase appearing only in this revised version of the original remark [JMN, VIII, 405]) and "turns the world to glass" (W, III, 12, 42, 20).

The poem joining the darkness of sensation and the light of thought evinces a dynamic twilight or metamorphic act of transition. Moreover, the season of Spring with its suggestion of thaw, renewed brightness, and the return of singing birds provides Emerson with a chief source of imagery (in conjunction with the vehicular horse and goat's legs) to depict life's principle of flux or metamorphosis which the poet brings to light. Since "the quality of [his] imagination is to flow, and not to freeze," the poet stimulates, as a Springlike force, the impulses beneath the rigid forms with which men encase their lives: "the metamorphosis of things into higher organic forms is their change into melodies"; "new passages are opened for us into nature; the mind flows and through things hardest and highest, and the metamorphosis is possible" (W, III, 34, 25, 27).

The metamorphic ascent only occurs when man maintains a fluid or ceaseless interaction between sensation and thought. This idea Emerson poetically depicts in the final sentence of the essay, in the same passage in which he speaks of beauty (and by implication the poet's song) as the dynamic transition between night and day.

In this passage he also notes that beauty resides "wherever snow falls or water flows or birds fly" (W, III, 42). The images, carefully rearranged from their previous order in the original journal entry (JMN, VIII, 405), summarize as no other means of writing could have in quite the same way, much of what Emerson has depicted throughout the essay. Not only does each image suggest motion but the direction of its implied motion is pertinent. The snow falling downward from the heavens represents the descent of the thought which will become the new ground or form; the birds flying upward from the earth symbolize the countering impulse ascending through form. Both meet and interact in the metamorphic, fluid point signified by flowing water. Looked at from a simpler but related perspective, in the human self Winter with its frozen forms and Spring with its return of avian impulse both contribute to a single dynamic cycle involving their ceaseless interaction in the metamorphic moment of thaw, which (like the will) is nothing more than the action resulting from interplay between two extremes.

In producing this dynamically unifying melody of the song, the poet evidences integration of the Panlike features of human nature. Like Pan, furthermore, the poet eventually entices men through his music: "He is isolated among his contemporaries by truth and by his art, but with this consolation in his pursuits, that they will draw all men sooner or later" (W, III, 5). In the meantime he "must pass for a fool and a churl for a long season," even as Pan suffers from an erroneous reputation in Emerson's opinion. In fact, however, this reputation "is the screen and sheath in which Pan has protected his well-beloved flower" (W, III, 41–42; Pan is not mentioned in the original version of this comment [JMN, VIII, 405]). During the long wintry season the poet, like Pan, protects the blossom of Spring, the song or melody symbolizing the achievement of man's upper region—"the flower of the mind" (W, III, 27).

Through their enchanting music, poets become Panlike "liberating gods" touching us "by a wand which makes us dance" (W, III, 30), an activity involving the interaction of feet and head. Such an integration of wild impulse and disciplined form (dancing) puts man in harmony with the natural scheme of things, in accord with which the seasons of the self recapitulate the dancing or fluid moment of thaw between Winter and Spring.

Emerson extends the image of "liberating gods" in the essay when he speaks of the poet as the individual who enables men to escape by providing the key to unlock the prison of thought (W, III, 33). In doing so, the poet not only discloses man's "common wealth" but also, as a representative of man, indicates that everyone is "a sovereign," an "emperor" with "tyrannous eye," a "true land-lord! sea-lord! air-lord!" (W, III, 5, 7, 37, 42). In revealing man's divinity, that part of the Panlike self so often unexpressed, he converts what seems "ignoble" into a new nobility (W, III, 42) based on integration of the sea (impulse), land (will), and air (thought) features of the self. Under his enchantment men become "the children of music" (W, III, 9) or young Pans; for, Emerson playfully remarks, "we are not pans . . . of the fire and torch-bearers, but children of the fire, made of it, and only the same divinity transmuted and at two or three removes, when we know least about it" (W, III, 4).

Emerson's development of Pan as the central hieroglyph

in "The Poet" is one of the most brilliant and original expressions of his artistic technique. At the very least, it provides a unique variation of his concept of the Logos-like nature of the human self. "O what are heroes, prophets, men," Emerson asks in a poem, "but pipes through which the breath of Pan doth blow / A momentary music" (W, IX, 360).

V

Lofty Ballooning and Other Hieroglyphs

This final chapter discusses several miscellaneous hieroglyphs which Emerson used again and again in such a manner that it would not be profitable to devote entire sections to each one separately. Generally, with the notable exception of the one unifying "Fate," these central hieroglyphs prove less satisfying than those previously studied because they are less complexly developed. Several, in fact, are successful minor supportive motifs in the essays already discussed. But they are not without interest in themselves or in the further illumination they cast on Emerson's artistic practice. With the exception of "Fate," my exegesis of these essays is less thorough than that of others in this book. It focuses on aspects not extensively treated elsewhere and on aspects I believe to be particularly revealing with regard to Emerson's artistry.

"Prudence"

The central hieroglyph and its motifs in "Prudence" (1841), not the most artistically provocative of Emerson's writings, appear in minor roles in other essays. The work is instructive, however, in its explicit comments touching Emerson's aesthetic ideas.[1] Furthermore, because it underwent less severe revision than did most of his early essays—"The Poet," for instance, contains few passages from the lecture with the same title (EL, III, 348–65)—"Prudence" can be carefully compared to its earlier version, delivered at the Boston Masonic Temple on January 17, 1838. This comparison provides an excellent opportunity to observe Emerson in the act of paring his rhetoric, polishing his phrases, and, most important, shaping his hieroglyph in terms of finely honed imagery.

The garden and the farm comprise the central images in "Prudence," though properly speaking they are treated as one hieroglyph. Even in the lecture stage of the essay this hieroglyph emerges, though Emerson had not yet fully developed the image of the garden. When revising the lecture he added references to the garden to both the introduction and the conclusion, thereby framing the original reference near the middle. In this new introduction, derived from a comment in one of his journals (JMN, VII, 421), the following passage appears: "I have no skill to make money spend well, no genius in my economy, and whoever sees my garden discovers that I must have some other garden" (W, II, 221). The other garden is "Prudence" as well as his other writings. Language provides the tools with which he actively tends this garden; for Emerson, as we have seen, language is a mode of action.

To reinforce this garden image and its implications Emerson also modified the penultimate paragraph of the essay. In the lecture, as in the 1837 journal entry from which the passage was derived (JMN, V, 346), Emerson had written: "If not the Deity but our wilfulness hews and shapes the new relations, their sweetness escapes, as strawberries lose their flavor by cultivation" (EL, II, 321). When including this passage in the essay, Emerson made a few changes, the most significant of which was replacement of the phrase "by cultivation" with "in garden-beds" (W, II, 240).

Although Emerson deliberately frames the essay with these garden images, he intends them to merge with the more prevalent farm imagery, a design reflected in a sentence appearing nearly midway: "His garden or his poultry-yard tells him many pleasant anecdotes" (W, II, 227). Similar references to farming, some of which equally apply to gardening, abound in "Prudence." Emerson speaks of the agriculturist; hard soil; roots; hay and the haymaker's rake; wheels, pins, and carts; oxen; barns; presses and corn chambers. Such recurring imagery helps depict the central hieroglyph informing Emerson's focus on human labor (the will), on the task of harvesting the fruits derived from what one has sown.

Verbs of action, use, or labor occur throughout. Significantly in his new introduction Emerson writes: "My prudence consists in avoiding and going without, not in inventing of means and methods, not in adroit steering, not in gentle repairing" (W, II, 221). This series of participles gives a sense of continuing action, a sense of a dynamic present; simultaneously the focus of the sentence narrows, moving from *inventing* to *steering* to *repairing*, so that one cannot escape an awareness of the increasing role of human hands. This inference prepares the reader for an emphasis throughout the essay on the fit employment of one's hands, an image which, as frequently remarked in this book, symbolizes proper exercise of the human will.

Emerson's use of hand imagery is indicative of his artistry in "Prudence." In an early passage in the essay he says of man: "Let him, if he have hands, handle"; instead of laboring futilely with "stupid hands," let him discover how to make his "hands grasp" until his best efforts join him "hand to hand" with his "friends and fellow workers" (W, II, 226, 228, 229, 238, 240). This series of hand images demonstrates Emerson's belief that all men should engage in the common work of individual self-fulfillment, which will in turn unite them in mutual fellowship. But he also develops this motif another way; near the end he uses previous references to man's hands both to avoid a mere abstraction and at the same time to convey the higher or spiritual dimension he always sought to unveil: "The natural motions of the soul are so much better than the voluntary ones that you will never do yourself justice in dispute. The thought is not then taken hold of by the right handle, does not show itself proportioned and in its true bearings" (W, II, 239). The total impact of these two sentences can be assessed only when we realize how, in passages cited previously, Emerson provided for this later appearance of the word *handle*. As a result this final reference to hands, symbolizing the transforming power of the will, now operates nearly subliminally, causing the mind of the reader to ascend involuntarily toward a higher perception beyond the implications of previous contexts in which the image was employed.[2]

The controlling hieroglyph instructs that one should learn to handle "the just fruit of his own labor" (W, II, 233)—be it garden produce or ripened thought. Man needs to recognize that "what he sows he reaps" (W, II, 235; also II, 232). This homiletic note links hand and garden-farm images. Throughout "Prudence" Emerson speaks of the work of hands in the garden or on the farm. He mentions the harvesting of fruits, the "whetting of the scythe," the "mower's rifle," the value of "husbanding little strokes of the tool," and the motions of hewing and shaping (W, II, 227, 228, 229, 234, 240). Furthermore, he writes of building a workbench or setting a tool box "in the corner of the barn-chamber, and stored with nails, gimlet, pincers, screwdriver and chisel" (W, II, 227). The union of garden-farm and hand motifs permits repeating the sort of effect achieved with the word *handle*. Near the end of "Prudence" he again drives home an idea which, without reinforcement by the foregoing images, would have remained abstract: "He who wishes to walk in the most peaceful parts of life with any serenity must screw himself up to resolution" (W, II, 237). The word *screw* (symbolizing the will) functions at a nearly subliminal level, conveying all previous hand and work images while slightly but significantly elevating the context of this imagery from that of the Understanding, which catalogues facts of the mundane world, to that of the Reason, which intuitively perceives the spiritual meaning of these facts.

This emphasis on employment of one's hands in suitable work informs another series of images concerning the ripeness of one's harvest. Avoiding either a premature or a tardy harvest lies very much at the heart of the explicit statement of "Prudence." Emerson remarks, for example, that one's "words and actions to be fair must be timely" (W, II, 228). To communicate the wastefulness of an immature harvest he again draws upon the garden-farm hieroglyph: "If the hive be disturbed by

rash and stupid hands, instead of honey it will yield us bees"
(W, II, 228). If, on the contrary, one learns to "accept and
hive" all the facts of his experiences (W, II, 226), then he can
prevent the pang of an abortive harvest. Extending these hive
and honey images in a manner similar to his use of the words
handle and *screw*, he writes: "If you believe in the soul, do not
clutch at sensual sweetness before it is ripe on the slow tree of
cause and effect" (W, II, 228); rather, "let us suck the sweetness of these affections and consuetudes that grow near us"
(W, II, 240).

Akin to the danger of an unseasonable harvest is a tardy
one. To some extent, Emerson advises, time must be spent
waiting; yet, "how much of human life is lost in waiting," how
often "life wastes itself whilst we are preparing to live" (W,
II, 235, 240). These two exclamations derive their literary
force from the motif of waste developed throughout the essay.
Early in "Prudence" Emerson laments that time "is slit and
peddled into trifles and tatters," that "scatter-brained and
'afternoon' men spoil much more than their own affair," and
that "we stand amidst ruins" (W, II, 225, 229, 231). Images
of decay from a delayed harvest similarly dominate a passage
not in the lecture version but later largely drawn from another
lecture (EL, II, 243; cf. JMN, V, 412) and added to the essay
to strengthen the internal pictorial structure:

> Iron, if kept at the ironmonger's, will rust; beer, if not brewed
> in the right state of the atmosphere, will sour; timber of ships
> will rot at sea, or if laid up high and dry, will strain, warp
> and dry-rot; money, if kept by us, yields no rent and is liable
> to loss; if invested, is liable to depreciation of the particular
> kind of stock. Strike, says the smith, the iron is white; keep the
> rake, says the haymaker, as nigh the scythe as you can, and
> the cart as nigh the rake.   (W, II, 234–35)

This last sentence proves especially useful because it contributes to and provides counterpoint for the scythe and hay
imagery planted in an earlier comment which, likewise not
present in the lecture,[3] stresses the timeliness of one's harvest:
"A gay and pleasant sound is the whetting of the scythe in the

mornings of June, yet what is more lonesome and sad than the sound of a whetstone or mower's rifle when it is too late in the season to make hay?" (W, II, 228–29). Lateness can result in the self's loss of thought, in the loss of the virtue (*vir*/man) of one's work or will, just "as strawberries lose their flavor in garden-beds" (W, II, 240).

On the other hand, Emerson explains through his garden-farm hieroglyph, man needs to learn when to be a "good hus-band," when to "brew, bake, salt and preserve," when to participate in the "harvesting of fruits in the cellar," for his future nourishment; or else, instead of nourishing him, his ac-tions and experiences will "usurp" and "eat up the hours" (W, II, 225, 226, 227).

That the timely harvest by man's hands, that the proper exercise of his will, should contribute to his nourishment and health is reinforced by references to bread. The first time Emerson introduces this image he does so at the level of means or utility, the lowest level of prudence and the one for which he expresses contempt; the elementary level of prudence wants to know "but one question of any project,—Will it bake bread?" (W, II, 223).

But Emerson soon undertakes the transformation of this image. When he writes that "we eat the bread which grows in the field" (W, II, 225), he reinforces his garden-farm hiero-glyph while also creates a burgeoning metaphor yoking man and nature. Wheat, not bread, grows; but in the spiritual cru-cible of the human will, in the action of the will's transforma-tion of the mulberry leaf (natural fact) into satin (thought) (CW, I, 96), nature and man's "handling" of nature become inseparable. So bread, in a physical and a spiritual sense, must be given its due (W, II, 234). Every man should exert his will in sowing and harvesting the wheat, which he also should transform into the nutritious bread of thought: "by diligence and self-command let him put the bread he eats at his own disposal, that he may not stand in bitter and false relations to other men" (W, II, 235). Although the image of bread initially appears at the level of means, its final occurrence functions at the level of the symbol which points "to the beauty of the thing signified" (W, II, 222).

As all of these images connote, either a premature or a late harvest of thought leads to the fate of the "imprudent genius" who falls "chilled, exhausted and fruitless" (W, II, 233). *Exhausted* refers to his ill health. *Fruitless* points to the under-nourishment and the poverty (the essay is replete with refer-ences to wealth, gains, dowries, rewards, and fortunes) which have led to his poor health. Because Emerson has stressed how the fruits of one's labor may either be wasted or be made to provide nourishment and wealth, he, with more effect than is at first obvious, can say of those who vainly argue about un-important matters: "not a thought has *enriched* either party" (W, II, 239; italics added). This statement did not appear in the lecture. It was added later, taken from an 1838 journal entry (JMN, VII, 25); clearly Emerson saw how the pictorial implication of the word *enriched* suited his purposes in the essay, especially in the light of several preparatory image clusters already noted. *Enriched*, like *handle* and *screw*, is meant to make a gentle but telling impression upon the inner eye of the reader.

By echoing and frequently transforming the dimension of his garden-farm imagery Emerson created a hieroglyph for "Prudence." This essay may lack a systematic development of explicit thought, but it does not want organization. Controlled image clusters, which often in their ultimate sense visually appeal beyond the conscious level and which always resolve themselves in terms of the underlying central emblem, supply internal order and structure. This method permitted Emerson to proffer the salutary bread of this thought-full essay to his readers. He wanted the essay itself to depict the best prudence, that which "is content to seek health of body by complying with physical conditions, and health of mind by the laws of the intellect" (W, II, 222); [4] for Emerson, the laws of the former are also the laws of the latter.

"Prudence" presents a number of other images which per-tain to the central hieroglyph but which, albeit not less intentional than those already discussed, generally do not occupy the visual center of the essay. These secondary images form atmospheric foreground; they disclose a sense of motion, a sense of the rhythmic flux of time. Specifically, these scattered images most often concern climate, accenting the seasonal and the diurnal cycles which provide an appropriate setting for Emerson's emphasis on a timely harvest. That Emerson frequently refers to these and other cycles is clear from previous discussions in this book; but attention should be directed to the fact that in "Prudence" this sense of flux and flow was meant both to make the central hieroglyph and the truth it symbolizes intuitively more conspicuous to the reader's inner eye and to prevent the hieroglyph from emerging into perfect focus.

References to an "abundant flow" between "every suburb and extremity," to "swimming and oscillating" appearances, to a "swarming population," and to "the flow of wit and love" (W, II, 227, 229, 236, 239) suggest this fluid foreground. More successful in conveying a sense of this flux is an unassertive motif based on the cycle of the seasons: "we are poisoned by the air that is too cold or too hot, too dry or too wet" (W, II, 225); "summer will have its flies" (W, II, 225); "four months of snow make the inhabitant of the northern temperate zone wiser" (W, II, 226); "in the rainy day he builds a work-bench" (W, II, 227); "a gay and pleasant sound is the whetting of the scythe in the mornings of June" (W, II, 228); "in skating over thin ice our safety is in our speed" (W, II, 235); "the sun shines and the rain rains for both" (W, II, 238); "the terrors of the storm are chiefly confined to the parlor and the cabin. The drover, the sailor, buffets it all day, and his health renews itself at as vigorous a pulse under the sleet as under the sun of June" (W, II, 237).

As usual Emerson alludes to the diurnal cycle. Man's life, Emerson explains, remains "attached in nature to the sun and the returning moon and the periods which they mark" (W, II, 224); "there revolve, to give bound and period to his being on all sides, the sun and moon, the great formalists" (W, II, 225). Later in the essay Emerson writes: "Let him esteem Nature a perpetual counsellor, and her perfections the exact measure of our deviations. Let him make the night night, and the day day" (W, II, 234).

The rhythmic process or motion implied by these secondary images furnishes a medium for the ascendancy of the structuring hieroglyph of "Prudence." Vivian Hopkins has rightly noted that, for Emerson, "when the creative imagination works . . . it first perceives the *flowing* beneath the apparently *fixed* quality of things, and then reproduces that quality in a finished work." [5] One needs to add that this fluidity, as exemplified in "Prudence," finally urges the reader's mental eye of Reason to seize, by way of contrast, upon the governing hieroglyph as a steady point of reference, even while that same fluidity forces this perception continually to struggle for a clearer focus on the spiritual truth symbolized by the hieroglyph. In this manner Emerson imparts a sense of the healthy transforming and evolutionary power of the will, which perpetually metamorphoses the dimly perceived absolute truth of spiritual facts into the ever-elusive clarity of focused thought.

The following passage from "Prudence" not only partakes of the climate motif but also explains how Emerson uses language in the essay:

> How many words and promises are promises of conversation! Let his be words of fate. When he sees a folded and sealed scrap of paper float round the globe in a pine ship and come safe to the eye for which it was written, amidst a swarming population, let him likewise feel the admonition to integrate his being across all these distracting forces, and keep a slender human word among the storms, distances and accidents that drive us hither and thither, and, by persistency, make the paltry force of one man reappear to redeem its pledge after months and years in the most distant climates.   (W, II, 235–36)

According to this statement, language, the "slender human word" derived through the human will, represents more stability than the flux surrounding it. The image *slender* intimates the fragility of language in this environment, but the image's implication of linearity also typifies precisely how a central hieroglyph is supposed to function. This procedure embodies the artistic complement to what Sherman Paul has observed as Emerson's aim: "that of erecting the vertical standard of value perpendicular to the horizontal enslaving his day." [6] When man stands erect his words will reflect his condition, integrating his being by transforming the facts at his feet, through his will, into expressed thought. Such upright, *virtuous* words and actions (for actions are also words) will convey wisdom; and, appropriately, "wisdom will never let us *stand* with any man or men on an unfriendly *footing*" (W, II, 240; italics added).

As his use of the One Man hieroglyph indicates, the image of verticality is important to Emerson. In "Prudence," too, perpendicularity becomes a pivotal image. By citing a long quotation from the art criticism of the Grand Duke of Weimar, Emerson not only contributes further to the primary image clusters reinforcing the hieroglyph in "Prudence" but also emphasizes the earlier phase of his motif of the standing man and provides another clue as to how he practiced the art of language:

> "I have sometimes remarked in the presence of great works of art, and just now especially in Dresden, how much a certain property contributes to the effect which gives life to the figures, and to the life an irresistible truth. This property is the hitting, in all the figures we draw, the right centre of gravity. I mean the placing the figures firm upon their feet, making the hands grasp, and fastening the eyes on the spot where they should look. Even lifeless figures, as vessels and stools—let them be drawn ever so correctly—lose all effect as soon as they lack the resting upon their centre of gravity, and have a certain swimming and oscillating appearance. The Raphael in the Dresden gallery (the only great affecting picture which I have seen) is the quietest and most passionless piece you can imagine; a couple of saints who worship the Virgin and Child. Nevertheless it awakens a deeper impression than the contortions of ten crucified martyrs. For beside all the resistless beauty of form, it possesses in the highest degree the property of the perpendicularity of all the figures." This perpendicularity we demand of all the figures in this picture of life. Let them stand on their feet, and not float and swing.   (W, II, 229–30)

Amid the "swarming and oscillating" which (as the secondary images intimate) constitute life's condition, men, the central farmer figures in Emerson's "Prudence" portrait, should rise and stand "firm upon their feet," just as the central hieroglyph emerges in an essay. Emerson did not want anyone to "lose his balance" or to "stand in bitter and false relations to other men" (W, II, 224, 235). Rather, by aiming at both the conscious and the unconscious of his readers, Emerson sought to place man on a "convenient footing" of friendship (W, II, 237). Through the artistic management of the garden-farm hieroglyph, Emerson sought to convey to his readers an impression of their center of gravity, an impression of how it feels to stand erect in self-reliance and thereby achieve "the art of securing present well-being" (W, II, 240; note the image of health).

If the magic of Emerson's slender human word, as it ascends or expands its contexts and implications beyond the utilitarian level of common sense and even the poetic level of taste, if the artistry of the aesthetic device of the stable yet elusive hieroglyph has done its work, then the "spiritual perception" of the reader's inner eye momentarily glimpses "the beauty of the thing signified" (W, II, 222).

"Intellect"

The diurnal cycle providing the foreground of "Prudence" and appearing in numerous other essays, particularly "Self-Reliance" and "Experience," serves as the central hieroglyph in "Intellect" (1841). Therefore, I would bypass the work were it not that in the essay Emerson makes several remarks touching on his aesthetic practice. In "Intellect" Emerson considers the relation between his notion of the intellect, which as "the simple power anterior to all action or construction" pierces form, and his notion that the thought of the intellect requires "a vehicle or art": "To be communicable it must become picture or sensible object" (W, II, 325, 335). Because the intellect dissolves laws and method even though it uses and depends on them, a tension arises whenever pictorial forms of art are employed to express the "intellect constructive" and to communicate to the "intellect receptive." [7] This tension is most evident in "The Poet," where we noted Emerson's emphasis on how the sensible expression of an idea corresponds to the level of form and sensation, which the healthy process of the intellect should continually dissolve to provide for new thought.[8]

Emerson's awareness of this tension urged him to construct for "Intellect" a hieroglyph which provides a vehicular image without demanding tangible reality for itself, one which by its very nature suggests the process of creation and dissolution. In choosing the traditional image of light and darkness as his hieroglyph, he neatly avoided making his picture too concrete; for both features, though sensible, remain elusive insofar as each depends on the other for its reality and insofar as neither is readily reducible to a simple level of human sensation—one reason these same images appealed to Emerson's New England Puritan ancestors. They were generally alert to avoid imagery which in its tangibility drew too much attention to itself and consequently distracted hearer or reader from the sense or meaning it was to communicate. Images of light and darkness also permitted Emerson to allude to the diurnal cycle, thereby suggesting the dynamic interaction between imagery and the intellect.

A characteristic passage implying several aspects of Emerson's use of this hieroglyph occurs early in the essay:

> If you gather apples in the sunshine, or make hay, or hoe corn, and then retire within doors and shut your eyes and press them with your hand, you shall still see apples hanging in the bright light with boughs and leaves thereto, or tasselled grass, or the corn-flags, and this for five or six hours afterwards. There lie the impressions on the retentive organ, though you knew it not. So, lies the whole series of natural images with which your life has made you acquainted, in your memory, though you know it not; and a thrill of passion flashes light on their dark chamber, and the active power seizes instantly the fit image, as the word of its momentary thought.   (W, II, 333–34)

At one level this passage indicates that light and darkness merely comprise two phases of a single unit. At another level it defines and demonstrates how, in Emerson's opinion, the intellect functions, how spontaneous impulse or passion is stimulated by the retained image and then is transformed through "the active power" (the will) in order to produce the expression (word) of a new momentary thought. Emerson intends his aesthetic device of the hieroglyph to flash, like the stimulus of light, upon the darkness of the reader's memory. While picturing some seemingly trivial fact, such as that of the diurnal cycle, the hieroglyph illuminates every fact symbolized so that it "revisits the day, and delights" (W, III, 332). In short, by means of the lightlike stimulus of a hieroglyph, some mundane fact buried in the darkness of memory suddenly participates in a mental cycle akin to the diurnal one of nature. When released from darkness, when it revisits the day, this fact gives light (delights). It then serves as a new illumination or stimulus, generating still another flash upon the darkness of memory and as the uniqueness of its light dies (completing an internal diurnal cycle) giving rise to a new image which perpetuates the process.

"Intellect" is replete with imagery pertaining to this internal diurnal cycle. In one noteworthy instance Emerson remarks, "You cannot with your best deliberation and heed come so close to any question as your spontaneous glance shall bring you, whilst you rise from your bed, or walk abroad in the morning after meditating the matter before sleep on the previous night" (W, II, 328; the last ten words, emphasizing Emerson's point, do not appear in an earlier version of the comment [EL, II, 250]). This momentary, spontaneous, enlightened glance is like the flash of "an alarming meteor" (W, II, 344), a brief impulse in the darkness of the self stimulating the will or active power into further illuminating thought. But just as the meteor's light must fade and just as every new morning must pass into the undifferentiated light of day, so each new thought must participate in an internal diurnal cycle. "Out of darkness" a thought comes "insensibly into the marvellous light of today," Emerson writes, just as the alarming meteor soon becomes "one more bright star shining serenely in your heaven and blending its light with all your day" (W, II, 327, 344).[9]

As a result, an endless balance exists between "intellect receptive," the nightlike process of recording facts, and "intellect constructive," the daylike process of expressing or illuminating facts (W, II, 334–35). That the act of transition between the two, that the exercise of the will,[10] be balanced is crucial; for the "truth of thought is . . . vitiated as much by too violent direction given by our will, as by too great negligence" (W, II, 328).

Moreover, when individuals reflect the proper proportion or balance evident in the diurnal cycle, their relations with others externally demonstrate this interaction between "intellect receptive" and "intellect constructive." "One soul is a counterpoise to all souls," Emerson explains, "a true and natural man contains and is the same truth which an eloquent man articulates" (W, II, 344, 343). But whereas the true hearer (intellect receptive) exalts because a momentary light has illuminated his inner darkness, the speaker (intellect constructive) laments because the flash of his insight must now pass away: "if I speak, I define, I confine and am less" (W, II, 342). But a natural balance is effected whenever "the waters of the great deep have ingress and egress to the soul" (W, II, 342).[11]

As a writer, Emerson strove for this sort of equilibrium. He could not be too vague or abstract, and at the same time he could not select vehicular imagery which proved too specific or concrete. "The power of picture or expression," Emerson explained regarding his use of hieroglyphs, "implies a mixture of will, a certain control over the spontaneous states" (W, II, 336). Without the active power or the will, the spontaneous impulse would never be metamorphosed into thought.

The problem of "a certain control" lies precisely at the heart of the tension in "Intellect." Just as Emerson wanted to fashion imagery stimulating to the intellect, which actually penetrates and dissolves the form represented by any image, so too he wished to integrate the antithetical forces of spontaneity and discipline. Art embodies the act of transition between the two forces. By selecting the diurnal cycle and, in particular, by emphasizing light—reusing in a creative manner an image traditionally applied to the Holy Spirit—Emerson tried to convey a sense of this transition. He allowed his light imagery only a suggestive or "flashing" presence. By creatively reemploying the image, Emerson assumed the role of an artistic Diogenes, whose acquired truth "is a lantern which he turns full on what facts and thoughts lay already in his mind" (W, II, 332). Emerson's art was designed to teach others to "get a lamp" so that they could "find the man who can yield him truth" (W, II, 333, 342).

"History"

The peripheral reference to stars in "Intellect" is expanded to major proportions in "History" (1841), in which the zodiac serves as the central hieroglyph. Emerson speaks of the common attitude toward history as a superstitious respect, akin to the feelings some people have about astrological implications of the zodiac. As a result, he indicates, men have allowed themselves to be tyrannized by the specific facts of history, never realizing that, like the zodiac, history actually is fiction. There can be no doubt, Emerson argues, that the facts of history, like the legends of mythology and the stars of the zodiac, "do exert a specific influence on the mind" (W, II, 33), but that influence should not accentuate human helplessness. Instead it should engender insight: "as crabs, goats, scorpions, the balance and the waterpot lose their meanness when hung as signs in the zodiac, so I can see my own vices without heat in the distant persons of Solomon, Alcibiades, and Catiline" (W, II, 5). All facts are malleable to human insight, even as is nature, in which "nothing is so fleeting as form" (W, II, 13–14).

The Proteus element of the self, that force which can "bend the shows of things to the desires of the mind" (W, II, 34), creates fictions or fables out of facts. Then it elevates them (figuratively in mythology, literally in astrology) to a "lofty sight where facts yield their secret sense" (W, II, 9). With regard to the magical influence of this secret sense and to his hieroglyph, Emerson asks: "Who cares what the fact was, when we have made a constellation of it to hang in heaven an immortal sign?" (W, II, 9).

Emerson's point concerning the nature of the influence of history, myth, and astrology is important because finally it presupposes a circularity (*zodiac* means *circle*) so prevalent in his thinking. If, the argument goes, these three features of man's world (history, myth, and zodiac) exert an influence on him and if they are the creation of his Protean self, then he influences himself. Varying an idea in "The American Scholar," that there is creative reading as well as creative writing, Emerson concludes that the "human mind wrote history, and this must read it" (W, II, 4). One's mind encounters a statement of fact (a creation of another mind) and from it should create still another statement of fact (another fiction), which returns to influence the human mind. This is why a person should not be passive before the influence of the zodiac-like facts of history; such facts derive from people like himself. Because man is thus the activator of his own influence and the originator of its subsequent insight, he is liberated instead of tyrannized by the alleged facts or fictions of history, mythology, and the zodiac. This insight establishes the context for Emerson's humorous remark in the opening paragraph of the essay that "what at any time has befallen any man, he can understand," a comprehension making him "a freeman of the whole estate" (W, II, 3). What *befalls* man through history or under the influence of the stars paradoxically frees him in the sense that by being his own influence toward further thought, liberated from the tyranny of specific facts, he becomes a freeman (free man/ citizen) participating in the entire sequence as both object and subject. Near the conclusion of the essay Emerson repeats his humorous reversal of the common view of astrological influences when he refers to the man who "sees the principle" (Emerson's usual pun on *prince* applies) and "refuses the *dominion* of facts," a man who after "much revolving" these facts like a zodiac in his mind "writes out freely his humor" (W, II, 33; italics added). In creating fictions, then, man liberates himself from the mean fact, even as the creatures in the zodiac lose their mundane specificity. In doing so, man influences his own humors in a manner popularly attributed to the stars. Proper history, it follows, is akin to "divining" in astrology: "every history should be written in a wisdom which divined the range of our affinities and looked at facts as symbols" (W, II, 40). For Emerson, "the thought is always prior to the fact; all the facts of history preëxist in the mind as laws" (W, II, 3).

In "History" Emerson develops the circularity of the zodiac and its representation of man's self-influence by varying the church motif also present in "Self-Reliance" and "The Over-Soul." Man's portrayal of the zodiac on the dome of the heavens is equivalent to the creative expression on the dome of St. Peter's Cathedral because nature is the true church after which such houses of worship are designed (W, II, 17, 20–21). But since the facts of nature derive from the human mind, man, who projects his religious disposition into nature, is the ultimate "Temple of Fame" (W, II, 38). The religious sentiment originating from man's inner temple is reflected in the cathedral of nature (in manifestations exemplified by astrological notions). This way man steadily advances toward a "lofty sight [elevated into fable or myth / moved closer to heaven, as if in a loft of a church] where facts yield their secret sense."

"The path of science and of letters is not the way into nature" (W, II, 40–41), it follows, because they are based on forms and do not adequately allow for the instinct which sparks religious awe and penetrates the "secret sense." Astrology, on the other hand, blends fact and fiction—hence Emerson's use of the zodiac as a central hieroglyph. He did not believe in astrology in the conventional sense, as this essay and an earlier one entitled "Demonology" (EL, III, 151–71) make very clear; he especially rebuked the tendency of some people to feel helpless under its influence.[12] However, he saw in astrology a reverential attitude and expression which should typify man's response to life.

The genuine artist captures this magical dimension of facts "by a deeper apprehension, and not primarily by a painful acquisition of many manual skills" (W, II, 17). This remark, with its reference to hands suggested by the words *manual* and *apprehension* (*ad* + *prehendere*), intimates the proper exercise of the will integrating instinct and thought. The word *apprehension*, with its double meaning of "to fear" and "to know," expresses the will (symbolized by the word's implied hand image) as the integration of instinct (to be feared respectfully because it is unknown and—note the ironic hand image—"out of reach of the understanding" [W, II, 15]) and of thought (which makes something known).

In the word *apprehension* Emerson poetically summarizes the entire point of the zodiac and its astrological implications as the hieroglyph in "History." The artist and the historian, in a sense, are to be astrologers transforming fact into fiction and thereby influencing their fellow men. As representative men, they function through their artistry and their historical accounts in a way similar to the zodiac; they become components in the process whereby man circularly influences himself.

"Poetry and Imagination"

A late essay, "Poetry and Imagination" (1875), seems to show some decline in Emerson's artistic control. In 1872 it was already in proof sheets, which even in 1875 Emerson still was trying unsuccessfully to revise. No certain conclusions about Emerson's art should be drawn from the essay because its final form derived from the editing of James Eliot Cabot, who selected and arranged all essays eventually published in *Letters and Social Aims*. Cabot, for instance, objected to what he considered needless repetition in the proof copy of "Poetry and Imagination," which he subsequently revised. This revision becomes a sensitive matter for the critic because in the essay Emerson speaks of the value of skillful reiteration, in one instance noting that architecture pleases through "the repetition of equal parts in a colonnade" (W, VIII, 45, 47–48). In the light of how frequently Emerson includes in his works explicit remarks relating to his artistic practice and of how

many ways he incorporates poetic techniques in his essays—
in "Poetry and Imagination" he asserts that "there are also
prose poets" (W, VIII, 50)—it might be suspected that he
intentionally was experimenting with the refrain as an archi-
techtonic device. Our suspicions increase when we observe
Emerson's somewhat too elaborate, self-conscious demonstra-
tion throughout the essay of his belief that one "cannot utter a
sentence in sprightly conversation without a similitude" (W,
VIII, 11).

Even with proper cautions in mind, however, this essay
provides some insight into the decline of Emerson's artistic
practice. The refrain effect, if it were intended as such, seems
a less satisfactory means of emphasis than his former proce-
dures. A refrain is basically static, though Emerson's usual
method of echo or reiteration, involving a slightly mutated
context which results in a new or elevated insight (such as his
play on the words *handle, screw,* and *enriched* in "Prudence"), influences his interpretation of the refrain. Likewise,
the central hieroglyph of "Poetry and Imagination" is not very
richly developed in its imagistic implications, a weakness un-
likely to be solely the result of Cabot's editing. In fact, the
bareness of the hieroglyph is somewhat reminiscent of Emerson's early lectures, which tend to center on loosely related
image clusters.

In accord with his belief that one cannot speak well other
than in similitudes and that an audience delights in an image
(W, VIII, 12), Emerson structures "Poetry and Imagination"
around the hieroglyph of the child. The poet, Emerson writes,
is "like a delighted boy" for whom nature is a house or, more
accurately, a "magnificent hotel" where he looks about with
"fascinated eyes" (W, VIII, 53, 4, 19). For him the stars are
toys, and his perception of creation, which "is on wheels,"
serves as a "go-cart" for his further discernment of how "power
and purpose ride on matter to the last atom" (W, VIII, 3, 4,
5). This perception deepens in the poet's childlike imagination,
in that part of him "ever attended by pure delight" and ever
influencing his fascinated eyes (W, VIII, 18). What delights—

the refrain aspect of this word should not be overlooked—the imagination of the poet similarly pleases an audience: the image. Appropriately, then, the world represents not only a toy but also "an immense picture-book" (W, VIII, 9) for the child-like poet. Nature does not provide the only material for the illustrations in this book; human deeds contribute as well, for "a man's action is only a picture-book of his creed" (W, VIII, 23).

Even these few remarks demonstrate that management of the hieroglyph in this essay, at least in the version as it now appears, is not as consistent or as complex as that in many of his earlier writings. Nevertheless, Emerson does try to prevent the governing image from becoming too simplistic and static by indicating that, whereas ideally man should retain certain childlike features throughout his life, he should not remain fixed at one stage of youthfulness. A time should arrive when men "no longer value rattles" and eventually "outgrow the books of the nursery" (W, VIII, 49, 68), particularly the picture books of past actions. Swedenborg's refusal to rid himself of "the dead scurf of Hebrew antiquity," for example, impresses Emerson as typical of the Scandinavian theologian's "boyish" aspect (W, VIII, 34–35). To adhere to facts of the past is to be "cribbed," to remain at the "cradle" level of perception (W, VIII, 37, 3). But if the cradle is utilized, like the go-cart, as a vehicular phase toward maturity, then man begins to see through these facts. He becomes a more advanced child. Then "the poetry which satisfies more youthful souls is not such to a mind like his, accustomed to grander harmonies;— this being a child's whistle to his ear" (W, VIII, 56).

Clearly Emerson uses the child image both positively and negatively. This does not result from any confusion in his old age; for, as we have noted elsewhere, throughout his essays he relies on the child image to define the best and the worst attributes of man. In "Poetry and Imagination" the hieroglyph portrays that ideally, without remaining immature generally, one should maintain a youthful imaginative fascination, the sort of response evident in the child who resents having a Cinderella doll revealed as "nothing but pine wood and rags" (W, VIII, 12). Thus, in Emerson's view, Swedenborg possessed the proper imagination yet remained cribbed regarding his ability to advance beyond a certain level of fact in his nursery book. In contrast, Michelangelo evinced the same sort of imaginative capacity, but because of his ever-inquisitive, maturing mind he never remained cradled in some specific level of fact: "The aged Michel Angelo indicates his perpetual study as in boyhood,—'I carry my satchel still' " (W, VIII, 14).[13] Ideally maturation advances one to a stage where he can recognize a fact of the past, whether a natural detail, a human action, or a poem, as a "child's whistle" and somehow does so without destroying an ongoing spirit of youthfulness: "nor must [we] console ourselves with prose poets so long as boys whistle and girls sing" (W, VIII, 52).

In short, Emerson suggests that ideally every person, at each level of maturation, should leave behind one phase of childhood for a new, more advanced one. Life should be, as Emerson intends Michelangelo's remark to indicate, a succession of childhoods. Maturation ought to be a paradoxical growth from childhood to childhood, and in this sense Emerson speaks of the distinction between youth and age as a deception (W, VIII, 14–15). As one abandons the specific facts of the nursery books of a former stage of growth, he takes the significance, the essential sign value, behind the pictures with him to the new phase.

At this ever-successive, deeper level of insight "the ballad and romance work on the hearts of boys, who recite the rhymes to their hoops or their skates if alone, and these heroic songs or lines are remembered and determine many practical choices which they make later" (W, VIII, 67). Beneath the heightened details of the ballad and of the romance lies an undercurrent of enchantment, an appeal most frequently sensed in the rhythm of the work (hence Emerson's image of boys reciting while using their hoops or skates). "Poetry is the perpetual endeavor to express the spirit of the thing" (W, VIII, 17), Emerson remarks, and particularly in the rhythm of a work can the spirit be felt alike by children and adults (older children). This is why, just as "the babe is lulled to sleep by the nurse's song," sailors and soldiers, at a more advanced stage of childhood, perform better in response to the rhythm of music (W, VIII, 46).

Increasing perception of this underlying spirit marks true maturation into advanced stages of childhood. In the evolutionary scheme as presented by John Hunter, Emerson notes, there is *"arrested and progressive development"* (W, VIII, 7).[14] Arrested development is shown in the person who is fascinated by the facts of nature's picture book (like the boy who "finds that his pocket-knife will attract steel filings" [W, VIII, 13]) or by past actions illustrating man's picture book but who never advances to a deeper fascination with the spiritual dimension underlying such facts. He remains cradled or cribbed and fails to use these facts as a go-cart to a new, more mature phase of childhood. In the case of the poet, arrested development means an inability to move from fancy to genuine imagination; for only the latter reads or penetrates forms to their essential spiritual truth (W, VIII, 15). We might conclude that Emerson sees each stage of an individual's existence as a transcendent refrain of childhood which somehow still advances the poem of his life. In this sense everyone is a poet (W, VIII, 25).

In its present form "Poetry and Imagination" is flawed, its central hieroglyph functionally strongest only in those parts drawn from a lecture written in 1854. Yet, even in such a late work Emerson reveals, however skeletally, the principal feature of his artistic technique. It is not difficult to imagine that, if he had been able to deepen and broaden the implication of his hieroglyph, particularly by integrating it more completely with subordinate motifs, "Poetry and Imagination" would rank with "Experience" and "The Poet" as an example of his finest essays. As it presently stands, however, it reveals wan flickerings of Emerson's former artistic brilliance.

"Fate"

"Fate" (1860) has long been recognized as one of Emerson's best essays, and I cannot think of a better essay with which to close this study of his artistic technique, unless it would be "Experience" or "The Poet," both already discussed.

The central hieroglyph of the essay is "the Dearborn balance" (W, VI, 14), which, next to that of Pan in "The Poet," is perhaps the most ingenious and accomplished of Emerson's aesthetic devices. The scale, symbolizing in the essay Emerson's belief that in the scheme of life "balances are kept" (W, VI, 37), is composed of two chief parts: a curved horizontal piece, from each end of which hangs a weighing pan, and a vertical support rising to the center of the crosspiece. This structure becomes Emerson's hieroglyph symbolizing the interplay between fate (synonymous in the essay to matter, nature, necessity, organization, and circumstance) and freedom (synonymous to mind, thought, liberty, character, and power). Apparent in the hieroglyph is the suggestion that a duality exists between man and nature, a shift from more optimistic attempts to assert a monistic relationship in earlier essays.

Emerson associates fate with the arc of the Dearborn balance and freedom with its vertical shaft in the first paragraph of "Fate." He remarks: "Our geometry cannot span the huge orbits of the prevailing ideas, behold their return and reconcile their opposition" (W, VI, 3). Living beneath an arc delineating human limitations, man cannot see the circle of which the arc is a part. The circumscription of prevailing ideas represents a mode of "tyrannical Circumstance" and, Emerson makes clear, "Circumstance is Nature" (W, VI, 14). Circumstance, as its literal meaning (*circum* + *stare*) suggests, includes everything which encircles man, everything which arcs over him in the scale of life and thereby defines the limits of his horizons. Specifically this image flashes in the statement that "a man's power is hooped in by a necessity which, by many experiments, he touches on every side until he learns its arc" (W, VI, 19–20).

A pan fraught with the weight of necessity hangs on each side of the arc of life's balance. With this feature of his hieroglyph in mind, Emerson speaks of how "avoirdupois weight" determines political elections and of how the Puritans "felt that the weight of the Universe held them down to their place" (W, VI, 14, 5). The weight of necessity makes the arc of the scales seem immovable, and most people, in Emerson's opinion, readily surrender their liberty when confronted by it. This observation becomes particularly ironic in his reference to political elections, for elections are supposed to be means whereby people assert their freedom rather than an illustration of abdication of freedom before the weight of circumstance.

When Emerson mentions "this mountain of Fate" (W, VI, 12), he amplifies his hieroglyph by finding a picture in nature which directly corresponds to it. In outline, a mountain looks like the arc of a Dearborn balance. That men live beneath the confines of the arced mountain just as they do beneath the arc of the scale becomes clear in Emerson's comment about certain delimiting evils which beset mankind: "These are pebbles from the mountain, hints of the terms by which our life is walled up" (W, VI, 19). When he remarks about the "adamantine bandages" confining man (W, VI, 17), Emerson intends to convey a brief glimpse of the mountain image. He combines the image of the mountain with that of the scale's arc when he comments that "high over thought, in the world of morals, Fate appears" (W, VI, 21).

Expanding the hieroglyph still further, Emerson likens the shape of the Dearborn balance and of the mountain to the configuration of the house. As we have seen in several earlier essays and as Emerson makes explicit in "The Snow-Storm" (1841) and in "Fate" (W, VI, 36–37), nature is the great house after which men model their homes. In the walls and arched roofs of these homes Emerson sees a reflection of the basic macrocosmic scale. Numerous allusions to this view of the house appear in "Fate," but the most specific instance of Emerson's equation of the house, the scale, and the mountain—

as if they were transparencies placed one upon another—occurs about midway: "We stand against Fate, as children stand up against the wall in their father's house and notch their height from year to year" (W, VI, 30).

Ingeniously Emerson once more extends his hieroglyph to include the shape of man, who, as we have noted several times previously, is himself the house of the spirit. Referring to the house, the mountains of nature, and to the human body, all correlatives for the macrocosmic scale, Emerson speaks of how "every spirit makes its house; but afterwards the house confines the spirit" (W, VI, 9). Similar to the mountains with their adamantine walls, "people seem sheathed in their tough organization" (W, VI, 9). In other words organization, as a mode of circumstance or necessity, tyrannizes over character, a mode of freedom (W, VI, 9). Each person, with his "dome of brow" (W, VI, 9), experiences individually what his race undergoes in the macrocosmic balance—a point Emerson makes by referring in a suggestive manner to correspondence between the contour of a fat man's body and that of the scale: "he has but one future, and that is already predetermined in his lobes and described in that little fatty face, pig-eye, and squat form" (W, VI, 11).

The reference to obesity in this passage as well as elsewhere suggests a human feature conforming to the accretion of weight in the pan of the macrocosmic scale and to the laying down of strata which broadens volcanic mountains. But Emerson argues that the horizontal broadening process with increased strata also should result in an upward progression. In other words, he identifies another kind of scale, one of ascent, with the vertical piece of the macrocosmic Dearborn balance. Emerson intimates this fact by noting that in evolution "the scale of tribes . . . is as uniform as the superposition of strata" (W, VI, 16). Ultimately Emerson's allusions to man's "potbelly" (W, VI, 9) or corpulence do not merely describe the similarity between the human outline and that of the mountain or balance, but equally indicate that to some extent man

has allowed his form to lose its shape, that he is not sufficiently
fit to provide the vertical muscular force which lifts the arched
weight of necessity.

Although man is rooted in matter or necessity, he possesses
a mind, the thoughts of which constitute his freedom: "So far
as a man thinks, he is free" (W, VI, 23). The capacity to think
makes man the vertical principle in the cosmic balance. This
notion informs Emerson's remark that, although man cannot
span the orbit of prevailing ideas, he does represent "a drag-
ging together of the poles of the Universe" and, as such a principle of verticality, he should "obey [his] own polarity" (W,
VI, 22, 3). Through man, the arc of fate is lifted upward along
the ascending evolutionary scale. His thought is the power
which is hooped (W, VI, 19); "thought dissolves the material
universe by carrying the mind up into a sphere where all is
plastic" (W, VI, 28). Emerson later similarly remarks in terms
of his mountain imagery, "if the wall remain adamant, it ac-
cuses the want of thought" (W, VI, 43). In accord with his
evolutionary role man should "burst the hoops and rive every
mountain laid on top" of him, penetrate upwardly the strata
of the arched walls of fate until he finds himself, Emerson
playfully explains, "suddenly mounted" in the majesty of his
power (W, VI, 34, 26).

In this sense man can extend the limits of his house, a correlative of the balance and the mountain. Although as a child
he is measured against the wall of his father's house, "when the
boy grows to man, and is master of the house, he pulls down
that wall and builds a new and bigger" one (W, VI, 30). As
he ages man grows upwardly. If he truly matures he rives the
mountainlike adamantine limits of prevailing ideas, the ideas
of his father and of the past. Emphasizing the word *loft*, meaning an upper room and suggesting man's proper ascent of the
strata of nature's mountain or house, Emerson subtly contributes to this aspect of his hieroglyph: "The right use of
Fate is to bring up our conduct to the loftiness of nature" (W,
VI, 24).

Man ascends to the loftiness of nature by thoughts from the

loft within his "dome of brow." The upward penetration of nature depends, in Emerson's view, on addition of new rooms in the upper story of the house that is man: "Now and then one has a new cell or camarilla opened in his brain,—an architectural, a musical, or philological knack" (W, VI, 11). A *camarilla* is a vaulted roof and, in this passage, refers to mental expansion pushing farther upward the arc of the macrocosmic balance, the sides of the mountain of fate, the walls of nature's house, and the limits of human flesh. "Man is the arch machine" or chief instrument for enlarging the upward limits of necessity and should not, it follows, be assessed "by his weight in pounds, or that he is contained in his skin" (W, VI, 17, 38).

That the hoop of necessity can never be broken, Emerson in this later phase of his thinking readily admits. One must have faith in "a just balance," he advises, and believe that "though we know not how, necessity does comport with liberty, the individual with the world, [one's] polarity with the spirit of the times" (W, VI, 4–5). In the macrocosmic scale pound balances pound, and so paradoxically "freedom is necessary": "If Fate follows and limits Power, Power attends and antagonizes Fate" (W, VI, 28, 23, 22). Man can only refine the limits of circumstance. The "ring of necessity is always perched at the top," Emerson explains, but its "limitations refine as the soul purifies" (W, VI, 20). Although "thought itself is not above Fate," the latter is a "limp band" which can be expanded (W, VI, 20–21). Such expansion may be man's only opportunity, but in the evolutionary scheme this capacity is everything. In "reaching, radiating, jaculating," power and freedom are asserted, and "the papillae of man run out to every star" (W, VI, 38). Such actions reveal that man, no longer perversely exemplifying the extendibility of nature's limits with a flabby pot-belly, possesses character or a backbone and so evinces a fit condition to stand erect and lift the weight of circumstance. Although the crosspiece of the scale, the sides of the mountain, the walls of the house, the skin of the body are always present, they remain subject to upward expansion by the human vertical principle at their center. Paradoxically the weight of these limits steadies the vertical principle. Emerson would have readily agreed with Augustine that weight does not necessarily tend toward the lowest place but toward the proper place.[15]

The emergence of a new camarilla in the mind is not, Emerson explains, confined to people in any particular profession. A scientist frequently manifests its occurrence in discoveries, such as that of the vertical principle of steam latent in water. Steam's upward movement demonstrates and provides another image of the evolutionary principle of lofty ascension informing the hieroglyph of "Fate." Steam can "lift pot and roof and carry the house away"; through human control this divine power can be made to lift "mountains, weight or resistance of water" (W, VI, 33–34). Like the scientist, a religious prophet can give expression to this power of human thought so as to "burst the hoops and rive every mountain laid on top of it," such as did "the broad ethics of Jesus" (W, VI, 6).

The professions of architecture and music likewise manifest these "noble creative forces" (W, VI, 25). Such architects as Christopher Wren and Georg Möller, in Emerson's opinion, expand the horizons of the former limits of design. Similarly, the ingenious musician makes use of the fixed scales (the pun is Emerson's) and from the tyranny of organization (an *organum* is a musical instrument) yields music. Man learns from the musician that, just as the weight of limits can give him stability, organization can also serve as an instrument of ascent: "The whole world is the flux of matter over the wires of thought to the poles or points where it would build" (W, VI, 44); "by obeying each thought frankly, by harping, or, if you will, pounding on each string, we learn at last" the power of freedom (W, VI, 4). When Emerson remarks that man should "show his lordship by manners and deeds on the scale of nature" (W, VI, 24), he plays on the interacting motifs of the musical scale, the evolutionary scale, and the macrocosmic scale or balance.

The poet represents a fifth profession which expresses the

noble creative force. The poet discerns the arc of matter in its darker (evening) and its lighter (dawn) aspects, as Emerson indicates in the poem introducing "Fate": "And on his mind, at dawn of day, / Soft shadows of the evening lay" (W, VI, 1). The poet speaks not only of the constricting rings of necessity but also of the promise of these same arcs as symbolized by the rainbow (W, VI, 41, 48). He urges others to discern the design imprisoning them. When he speculates, when he sees and thinks, he penetrates the design; for thinking is freedom, the assertion refining matter. The poet urges his fellow men to use "the windows of [their] eyes" (W, VI, 10) to see through the walls of necessity defining the limits of their present house. He promises men that "he who sees through the design, presides over it" (W, VI, 27). When men make this "ascending effort," this struggle "to lift [the] mountain of Fate," they engage in "a poetic attempt" (W, VI, 35, 12).

Emerson reiterates these points in another fashion in the essay. The poet, Emerson writes, reminds men to engage in *lofty ballooning;* he encourages them to ascend to the highest, most refined regions of nature through "loftiest ascensions" of thought in the upper story or brain of his fleshly house (W, VI, 21). Remarking that "the ruddered balloon" awaits man (W, VI, 32), Emerson poetically depicts the essential meaning of the hieroglyph of the Dearborn balance. The inflated balloon symbolizes the expandability of the arc of form by a principle of vertical power (free moving air or gas) and the steamlike ascension that results from the interaction of the two; the rudder suggests that the interaction is best effected through the integrating human will, which as frequently noted in our discussion of other essays, manifests the balanced interplay between impulsive freedom and rigid form. The ecstasy of life, Emerson implies in "Fate," lies in one's ability to participate in this activity of lofty ballooning: "now we are as men in a balloon, and do not think so much of the point we have left, or the point we would make, as of the liberty and glory of the way" (W, VI, 27). Man should not be concerned about the points of departure or arrival because these become arbitrary marks of diminishing distinction as expanding horizons are revealed to someone in an ascending balloon.

"Behind every individual closes organization," Emerson explains, and "before him opens liberty"; this dynamic process is as endless as the horizon expanding before the man in the rising balloon. Finally one must indeed conclude, albeit not from the pessimistic attitude the remark first seems to imply, that "our geometry cannot span these extreme points and reconcile them" (W, VI, 35, 4). The ecstasy of exerting the will, of always integrating freedom and necessity (like skating in "Experience," standing on a ball in "Nature," and sitting in "Self-Reliance"), is sufficient, as man ascends to the upper regions of lofty possibility.

Conclusion: The Slender Human Word

By making use of a picto-ideogrammatic configuration in such essays as "Fate," Emerson fulfilled his notion of the role of the poet. Everything "is and must be pictorial" (W, VI, 48; also VI, 26). The poet's function is to reveal the pictures in facts and words as well as to disclose the truth behind them. At its best a hieroglyph in an Emersonian essay not only serves as an emblematic nodal point coordinating several tangential motifs but also refines its own context to "ascend" increasingly with implications which, at an elusive instinctive level, stimulate the inner eye of the reader. The method of this expansion is not logical but, as we have seen, poetically associative, most often depending on pictures suggested by particular words and on a similarity of their design or outline. A hieroglyph becomes most genuine for Emerson when the picture it conveys readily integrates numerous aspects of life inherently or organically. Emerson designed the governing hieroglyph in an essay to transmit a total contextual pictorial effect rather than a distinctness of detail or relation.

Emerson made his finished essays appear effortless, almost as if he were speaking extemporaneously. Like the wary artist, he remarked in his notebooks (JMN, IV, 363), he removed the

scaffolding and left no clue to how he accomplished the wonder. Nevertheless, appropriate as such effortlessness is to his
notion of the poet as someone who remains close to instinct,
there can be no doubt that the aesthetic achievement of Emerson's best essays derives to a significant extent from conscious
artistic control.

Admittedly, Emerson tended to feel more comfortable with
the brief moments of insight recorded in his journals. When, for
instance, he was revising his work for *Essays: First Series,* he
complained: "I have been writing with some pains Essays on
various matters as a sort of apology to my country for my apparent idleness. But the poor work has looked poorer daily as
I strove to end it. My genius seemed to quit me in such a
mechanical work. . . . what I write to fill up the gaps of a
chapter is hard & cold, is grammar & logic; there is no magic
in it" (JMN, VII, 404–405).

Among other matters, Emerson feared the possibility that
he might become overly aware of the mechanics of structuring
an essay around a central hieroglyph. The magic, unconscious,
or inspirational aspect of his art, the impulse which revealed
to him the shimmery truth of a particular hieroglyph, might
vanish in the process of too much conscious control; for he
always believed that when the literary artist "sits waiting
inspiration he is a child, humble, reverent, watching for the
thoughts as they flow to him from their unknown source"
(JMN, V, 13).

Essentially Emerson's art conveys through the slender human word that dramatic moment between inspiration and
thought, that same transitional point of dynamic interaction he
time and again spoke of as the will. Significantly the central
hieroglyphs in his essays shimmer; in their flickering elusiveness and in their apparent endless expansion of context, they
never quite solidify but always ascend a little farther beyond
the reader's mental grasp. To the perceptive reader they impart a pictorial display and a sensation of the integration (will)
of instinct and thought. As a prose poet Emerson sought to
capture this perennial mystical moment. Too much concern

with architectonics might spoil the creative or ecstatic insights of his own mind as well as dissipate their potency for generating impulses in the mind of the reader; too little control equally signified a malfunction of the artist's will.

The best solution for Emerson was to concentrate on the overall effect of the hieroglyphic design, so that it would function in terms of visual and associative suggestiveness, not in terms of geometrically integrated details. In this regard he had noted of Michelangelo: "The things proposed to him in imagination were such that for not being able with his own hands to express so grand and terrible conceptions he often abandoned his work. This is the reason why he so often only blocked his statues" (EL, I, 110). Significantly, in a journal entry Emerson reflected, "May I say without presumption that like Michel Angelo I only block my statues" (JMN, V, 14). Emerson did not identify with Michelangelo's abandonment of his work but with the sculptor's respect for art as evident in his tendency to sketch. Like this artist and like the writers of ancient Greece, of whom he spoke in similar terms in *English Traits*, Emerson heeded his "designs, and less considered the finish" (EL, I, 108; W, V, 256). By developing an inherent central hieroglyph, ever-elusive in its ultimate context and implication, Emerson sought to convey the dynamic balance between the extremes of freedom and fate, instinct and thought, undisciplined vision and rigid artistry.

Considering his achievement, I think we should no longer deny Emerson his proper place among the artists, even more than among the thinkers, of nineteenth-century America. His essays are prose poems, as rich and complex as any modern literary critic might demand. In the past we have too frequently attended the ground tone of his essays. It is time we rise, the children of his music.

Acknowledgments

Every book incurs debts. I gratefully acknowledge my indebtedness to the Research Institute of the University of Texas at Austin for a grant enabling me to work on this book while I was on leave from the classroom; to my colleagues in the Department of English, University of Texas, for an invigorating sense of community, but especially to Joseph Moldenhauer and R. James Kaufmann for somehow finding the time to read the work while in manuscript; to Irwin C. Lieb, vice president and dean of graduate studies, University of Texas, for strong support; to William Bysshe Stein, guest editor of *ESQ: A Journal of the American Renaissance*, and to Carl T. Berkhout, editor of the *Notre Dame English Journal*, for publishing two brief earlier versions of parts of this study; to JoElla Doggett for generously assisting me editorially; and to Marion for understanding and encouragement beyond my due.

Notes

Preface

1. *The Life of Ralph Waldo Emerson* (New York: Scribner's, 1949), 278–79.

2. *The Imperial Self: An Essay on American Literature and Cultural History* (New York: Knopf, 1971), 49.

3. Santayana, *Interpretations of Poetry and Religion* (New York: Harper, 1957), 217–33; James, *Memories and Studies* (London: Longmans, Green, 1911), 19–34.

4. David F. Finnigan, "The Man Himself: Emerson's Prose Style," *Emerson Society Quarterly*, no. 39 (II Quarter 1965), 13. This essay is indebted to Vivian C. Hopkins, *Spires of Form: A Study of Emerson's Aesthetic Theory* (Cambridge: Harvard Univ. Press, 1951). See also Enno Klammer, "The Spiral Staircase in 'Self-Reliance,'" *Emerson Society Quarterly*, no. 47 (II Quarter 1967), 81–83.

5. Sidney P. Moss, "Analogy: The Heart of Emerson's Style," *Emerson Society Quarterly*, no. 39 (II Quarter 1965), 21–24.

6. Ronald Beck, "Emerson's Organic Structures," *Emerson Society Quarterly*, suppl. no. 50 (I Quarter 1968), 76–77.

7. Robert Lee Francis, "The Architectonics of Emerson's *Nature*," *American Quarterly*, 19 (Spring 1967), 39–52. Recently Barry Wood has discussed how *Nature* is dialectical in content and form: "The Growth of the Soul: Coleridge's Dialectical Method and the Strategy of Emerson's *Nature*," *PMLA*, 91 (May 1976), 385–97.

8. Sheldon W. Liebman, "The Development of Emerson's Theory of Rhetoric, 1821–1836," *American Literature*, 41 (May 1969), 178–206.

9. Jonathan Bishop, *Emerson on the Soul* (Cambridge: Harvard Univ. Press, 1964), pp. 101–43. Warner Berthoff, it might be noted, raises some objections to certain of Bishop's conclusions; see his introduction to a facsimile edition of *Nature* (San Francisco: Chandler, 1968).

10. Mary Worden Edrich, "The Rhetoric of Apostasy," *Texas Studies in Literature and Language*, 8 (Winter 1967), 547–60.

11. Roland F. Lee, "Emerson through Kierkegaard: Toward a Definition of Emerson's Theory of Communication," *English Literary History*, 24 (Sept. 1957), 229–48.

Chapter I

1. See, for instance, Paul Lauter, "Emerson's Revisions of *Essays* (First Series)," *American Literature*, 33 (May 1961), 143–58.

2. In his description of Emerson's system, Jonathan Bishop does not focus on the will. The will is present, however, in his remarks on moral sentiment (*Emerson on the Soul*, 66–72), for in Emerson's view the attainment or absence of a sense of virtue characterizes the will. I shall use the word *will* because Emerson used it and, moreover, because Emerson consciously makes use of traditions established by his Christian ancestors, for whom the concept of the will was most crucial.

Aspects of the system I detail are discussed by Leonard Neufeldt, "The Vital Mind: Emerson's Epistemology," *Philological Quarterly*, 50 (April 1971), 253–70; and J.A. Ward discusses the function of the will as both cause and effect in the conversion process in "Emerson and 'the Educated Will': Notes on the Process of Conversion," *English Literary History*, 34 (Dec. 1967), 495–517. Also helpful is Raymond Gardella's "In Emerson Consciousness Is King," *Emerson Society Quarterly*, no. 50 (I Quarter 1968), 5–9.

3. Sherman Paul writes of Emerson's notion of the artist: "One's store of everyday experiences becomes significant only when, in the moment of inspiration, it yielded the image by which insight could be expressed" (*Emerson's Angle of Vision: Man and Nature in American Experience*, Cambridge: Harvard Univ. Press, 1952, 119). Other studies on Emerson's concept of the artist include Nelson F. Adkins, "Emerson and the Bardic Tradition," *PMLA*, 63 (June 1948), 662–77; Percy W. Brown, "Emerson's Philosophy of Aesthetics," *Journal of Aesthetics and Art Criticism*, 15 (March 1957), 350–54; and Lawrence I. Buell, "Unitarian Aesthetics and Emerson's Poet-priest," *American Quarterly*, 20 (Spring 1968), 3–20.

4. See, for instance, my *The Will and the Word: The Poetry of Edward Taylor* (Athens: Univ. of Georgia Press, 1974), 76–77, 110–

12. My study concerns the seventeenth-century not the nineteenth-century Edward Taylor.

5. For other features of Emerson's view of his audience, see John H. Sloan, " 'The Miraculous Uplifting': Emerson's Relationship with His Audience," *Quarterly Journal of Speech,* 52 (Feb. 1966), 10–15; and Wendell Glick, "The Moral and Ethical Dimensions of Emerson's Aesthetics," *Emerson Society Quarterly,* no. 55 (II Quarter 1969), 11–18. Jeffrey Steinbrink suggests a relation between Emerson's sense of an audience and his view of fiction in "Novels of Circumstance and Novels of Character: Emerson's View of Fiction," *ESQ: A Journal of the American Renaissance,* 20 (II Quarter 1974), 101–10.

6. It is in this sense that we ought to bear in mind Gene Bluestein's observation that Emerson sought to produce "that moment of ecstasy in which a higher spiritual and emotional truth is perceived" ("Emerson's Epiphanies," *New England Quarterly,* 39, Dec. 1966, 455).

7. The following essays remark Emerson's use of proverbs: C. Grant Loomis, "Emerson's Proverbs," *Western Folklore,* 17 (Oct. 1958), 257–62; J. Russell Reaves, "Emerson's Use of Proverbs," *Southern Folklore Quarterly,* 27 (Dec. 1963), 280–99; Ralph C. LaRosa, "Emerson's Sententiae in *Nature,*" *Emerson Society Quarterly,* no. 58 (I Quarter 1970), 153–57; and LaRosa, "Invention and Imitation in Emerson's Early Lectures," *American Literature,* 44 (March 1972), 13–30. See also Emerson Grant Sutcliffe, *Emerson's Theories of Literary Expression* (Urbana: Univ. of Illinois Press, 1923), 39.

8. Ludwig Volkmann, in fact, has argued that emblems originated as an attempt to give contemporary expression to Egyptian hieroglyphics as they were understood in the writings of Pliny, Tacitus, Plutarch, Plotinus, and others (*Bilderschriften der Renaissance: Hieroglyphik und Emblematik in Ihren Beziehungen und Fortwirkungen,* Leipzig, 1923). Mario Praz notes that collections of proverbs and epigrams also played an important role in the spread of emblems (*Studies in Seventeenth-Century Imagery,* 2nd ed., Rome, 1964, 25–34); see also Don Cameron Allen, *Mysteriously Meant* (Baltimore: Johns Hopkins Univ. Press, 1970), 107–33.

9. While my book was in manuscript Irwin's "The Symbol of the Hieroglyphics in the American Renaissance" appeared in *American Quarterly,* 26 (May 1974), 103–26. The importance of this article lies mainly in alerting us to the fact that there was a wave of interest in Egyptian antiquity during the early nineteenth century and in tracing some implications of this interest (especially in

hieroglyphics) in the writings of Emerson, Thoreau, Hawthorne, and Melville. Irwin reasonably suggests that Emerson derived his knowledge of hieroglyphics from Jean François Champollion, Edward Everett, and Sampson Reed. Although Irwin correctly concludes that "in a sense, an Emersonian essay is simply the explication of a hieroglyphical emblem," he fails to realize that hieroglyphics must be concrete images and so mistakenly adds: "The emblem can be a human concept like history, an emotion like love, a virtue like prudence." Such notions are not hieroglyphs but the ideas hieroglyphs symbolize in some concrete image. Irwin's essay is nonetheless most welcome.

10. *Foreign Quarterly Review*, 21 (July 1838), 316–59. That this review may be a possible influence on Emerson's view of language, as expressed in "The Poet," is noted by Donald M. Murray, "Emerson's 'Language as Fossil Poetry': An Analogy from Chinese," *New England Quarterly*, 29 (June 1956), 204–15. Murray also indicates Emerson's familiarity with Marshman's prefatory remarks to *The Works of Confucius* and with an article in the *Asiatic Journal* (23 Aug. 1837, 280–81) on the Manchu mode of expressing the sounds of Chinese characters. Emerson's interest in the related matter of Egyptian hieroglyphics, albeit ignored by Murray, is equally evident; even as late as 1866, he borrowed from the Boston Athenaeum a book by Sir John Gardner Wilkinson entitled *The Egyptians in the Time of the Pharaohs*, which included a study of hieroglyphics (Kenneth Walter Cameron, *Ralph Waldo Emerson's Reading: A Corrected Edition*, Hartford: Transcendental Books, 1962, 114).

11. *Foreign Quarterly Review*, 339.

12. *The Enneads*, trans. Stephen MacKenna (London: Faber & Faber, 1969), 427. The influence of Plotinus on Emerson is discussed by John S. Harrison, *The Teachers of Emerson* (New York: Sturgis & Walton, 1910); Stuart Gerry Brown, "Emerson's Platonism," *New England Quarterly*, 18 (Sept. 1945), 325–45; and Arlen J. Hansen, "Plotinus: An Early Source of Emerson's View of Otherworldliness," *ESQ: A Journal of the American Renaissance*, 18 (III Quarter 1972), 184–85.

13. *The Apocalypse Revealed* (Philadelphia: Lippincott, 1875), 543–46. Emerson owned a copy of this book (Walter Harding, *Emerson's Library*, Charlottesville: Univ. of Virginia Press, 1967, 262). Swedenborg's influence on Emerson is well known, but see particularly Paul, *Emerson's Angle of Vision*; Kenneth Walter Cameron, "Emerson and Swedenborgism: A Study Outline and Analysis," *Emerson Society Quarterly*, no. 10 (I Quarter 1958), 14–

20; Clarence Hotson, "Emerson and the Swedenborgians," *Studies in Philology*, 27 (July 1930), 517–45; and Hotson, "Sampson Reed, A Teacher of Emerson," *New England Quarterly*, 2 (April 1929), 249–77.

14. See Norman A Brittin, "Emerson and the Metaphysical Poets," *American Literature*, 8 (March 1936), 1–21; J. Russell Roberts, "Emerson's Debt to the Seventeenth Century," *American Literature*, 21 (Nov. 1949), 298–310; Karl Keller, "From Christianity to Transcendentalism: A Note on Emerson's Use of the Conceit," *American Literature*, 39 (March 1967), 94–98.

15. (Cambridge, 1643), 1. Rosemary Freeman briefly notes the influence of Egyptian hieroglyphs on the emblematic tradition in England in *English Emblem Books* (London: Chatto & Windus, 1948), 40–41.

16. (London, 1638), 1.

17. In the eighteenth century, apparently some effort was made to distinguish differences; see Anthony, Earl of Shaftesbury, *Second Characters*, ed. Benjamin Rand (Cambridge: Cambridge Univ. Press, 1914), 90–94.

18. See Henry A. Pochmann, *German Culture in America, 1600–1900: Philosophical and Literary Influences* (Madison: Univ. of Wisconsin Press, 1957), 153–207; and Merrell R. Davis, "Emerson's 'Reason' and the Scottish Philosophers," *New England Quarterly*, 17 (June 1944), 209–28.

19. *Foreign Quarterly Review*, 330, 354–57.

20. See Edgar Wind, *Pagan Mysteries in the Renaissance* (New York: Norton, 1968), 17 and George Boas' introductory remarks to *The Hieroglyphics of Horapollo* (New York: Pantheon, 1950), 23–24. In *The Friend*, a book Emerson knew well, Coleridge refers to this tradition when he quotes from Rudolph von Langen: "But how are we to guard against the herd of promiscuous Readers? Can we bid our *books* be silent in the presence of the unworthy? If we employ what are called the *dead* languages, our own genius, alas! becomes flat and dead: and if we embody our thoughts in the words native to them or in which they were conceived, we divulge the secrets of Minerva to the ridicule of blockheads, and expose our Diana to the Actaeons of a sensual age" (*The Collected Works of Samuel Taylor Coleridge*, Princeton: Princeton Univ. Press, 1969, 1:51–52.

21. Harding, *Emerson's Library*, 150–51.

22. *Plutarch's Morals*, ed. William W. Goodwin (Boston: Little, Brown, 1870), IV, 72. Emerson owned only volumes I and IV of this edition, for which he had written the introduction. He also owned a complete five-volume set of the *Morals* (London: W. Tay-

lor, 1718); see Harding, *Emerson's Library*, 217–18 and Edmund Berry, *Emerson's Plutarch* (Cambridge: Harvard Univ. Press, 1961), 35–54, 229–31.

23. On Dionysus the Areopagite, whose name appears in Emerson's journals, see Wind, *Pagan Mysteries*, 12–13. Coleridge refers to the necessity of the symbol in *Biographia Literaria*, in *The Complete Works of Samuel Taylor Coleridge* (New York: Harper, 1871), 3:259–60.

24. In *Hieroglyphica* Valeriano argues that the techniques of Plato, Pythagoras, and Christ are indebted to Egyptian hieroglyphics (see Boas, *Hieroglyphics of Horapollo*, 39).

25. Charles Feidelson, Jr., in *Symbolism and American Literature* (Chicago: Univ. of Chicago Press, 1953), 122–34, remarks the inherent features of Emersonian paradox.

26. Plutarch indicates this function of the Sphinx in "Of Isis and Osiris" (see note 22).

27. Goethe's influence on Emerson is the subject of Frederick B. Wahr's *Emerson and Goethe* (Ann Arbor: George Wahr, 1915) and Vivian C. Hopkins' "The Influence of Goethe on Emerson's Aesthetic Theory," *Philological Quarterly*, 27 (Oct. 1948), 325–44.

28. Berthoff, p. vii. See also Leonard N. Neufeldt, "The Law of Permutation—Emerson's Mode," *American Transcendental Quarterly*, 21 (Winter 1974), 20–30.

29. *American Renaissance: Art and Experience in the Age of Emerson and Whitman* (London: Oxford Univ. Press, 1941), 64. See also Ralph C. LaRosa, "Emerson's Search for Literary Form: The Early Journals," *Modern Philology*, 69 (Aug. 1971), 25–35.

30. Lawrence I. Buell raises some interesting points about Emerson's effort to use yet conceal structure in "Reading Emerson for the Structures: The Coherence of the Essays," *Quarterly Journal of Speech*, 58 (Feb. 1972), 58–69.

31. Yukio Irie rightly comments that readers of Emerson's essays "might have closed the volumes with the impression that they had been in the realm of poetry" (*Emerson and Quakerism*, Tokyo: Kenkyusha, 1967, 90). Brian M. Barbour argues against the application of the term *poetic* to Emerson's prose in "Emerson's 'Poetic' Prose," *Modern Language Quarterly*, 35 (June 1974), 157–72.

Chapter II

1. Especially valuable are Henry Nash Smith, "Emerson's Problem of Vocation: A Note on 'The American Scholar,'" *New England Quarterly*, 12 (March 1939), 52–67; Stephen E. Whicher, *Freedom and Fate: An Inner Life of Ralph Waldo Emerson* (Philadelphia:

Univ. of Pennsylvania Press, 1953); and Merton M. Sealts, Jr., "Emerson on the Scholar, 1833–37," *PMLA*, 83 (March 1970), 185–95. Two notes of interest are John C. Broderick's "Emerson: Not Yet Clarified," *Emerson Society Quarterly*, no. 27 (II Quarter 1962), 24; and Robert H. Woodward's "Emerson's Cinder Metaphor in *The American Scholar*," *Emerson Society Quarterly*, no. 33 (IV Quarter 1963), 17.

2. "Emerson and the Organic Metaphor," *PMLA*, 69 (March 1954), 117–30. An earlier version of my remarks on Emerson's essay appeared as "Aspiring to the Highest: Imagery in Emerson's *The American Scholar*," *Notre Dame English Journal*, 8 (Fall 1972), 34–42.

3. Emerson's sense of humor has never been fully appreciated; but see Arthur M. Cory, "Humor in Emerson's Journals," *University of Texas Studies in English*, 34 (1955), 114–24; V. L. O. Chittick, "Emerson's 'Frolic Health,'" *New England Quarterly*, 30 (June 1957), 209–34; and Reginald L. Cook, "Emerson and the American Joke," *Emerson Society Quarterly*, no. 54 (I Quarter 1969), 22–27.

4. Consider also the pun on *ground* in "I have already shown the ground of my hope, in adverting to the doctrine that man is one" (CW, I, 65).

5. On the personal level, for Emerson, of this relation between action and thought, see Smith, "Emerson's Problem of Vocation," 52–67.

6. Cf. "Every man passes personally through a Grecian period. The Grecian state is the era of the bodily nature, the perfection of the senses . . . . The Greeks are not reflective, but perfect in their senses and in their health" (W, II, 24–25).

7. See especially Matthiessen, *American Renaissance*, 24–52; Hopkins, *Spires of Form*; Paul, *Emerson's Angle of Vision*; Alvan S. Ryan, "Emerson's *The American Scholar*," *Explicator*, 18 (June 1960), 53; Stephen Whicher, "Emerson's *The American Scholar*, Paragraph 6," *Explicator*, 20 (April 1962), 68; and Sacvan Bercovitch, "Emerson's *The American Scholar*, Paragraph 6," *Explicator*, 25 (Sept. 1966), 9.

8. In "The Head" (1837), Emerson wrote: "You have first an instinct, then an opinion, then a knowledge, as the plant has root, bud, and fruit" (EL, II, 251).

9. One should note, however, Joel Porte's argument that Emerson is intellectually more a man of the eighteenth century than one of the nineteenth (*Emerson and Thoreau: Transcendentalists in Conflict*, Middletown, Conn.: Wesleyan Univ. Press, 1966).

10. Sacvan Bercovitch, "The Philosophical Background to the

Fable of Emerson's 'American Scholar,' " *Journal of the History of Ideas*, 28 (Jan. 1967), 123–28.

11. See, for example, *The Golden Verses of Pythagoras*, trans. Fabre d'Olivet (New York: Putnam, 1925), 209. Emerson was very familiar with the teachings of Pythagoras.

12. At present the best discussion of the art in *English Traits* appears in Joel Porte's "The Problem of Emerson," *Uses of Literature*, ed. Monroe Engel (Cambridge: Harvard Univ. Press, 1973), 85–114.

13. For the autobiographical and political implications of Emerson's remarks in this essay, see Arthur I. Ladu, "Emerson Whig or Democrat," *New England Quarterly*, 13 (Sept. 1940), 419–41.

14. Typically Emerson employs the image of childhood negatively or positively as the occasion warrants. This fact should be kept in mind when reading Tony Tanner's assessment of the child image in Emerson's work (*The Reign of Wonder: Naivety and Reality in American Literature*, Cambridge: Cambridge Univ. Press, 1965, 41–44). See also Joseph Baim, "The Vision of the Child and the Romantic Dilemma: A Note on the Child-Motif in Emerson," *Thoth*, 7 (Winter 1966), 22–30.

15. Note, as well, Emerson's references to taxation which function as a part of this motif (W, III, 202, 215).

16. For a study of Biblical influences on Emerson, see Harriet R. Zink, *Emerson's Use of the Bible* (Lincoln: Univ. of Nebraska Press, 1935).

17. Compare Thoreau's pun on sleepers in *Walden* (Princeton: Princeton Univ. Press, 1971), 92–93.

18. LeRoy Lad Panek's "Imagery and Emerson's 'Compensation,' " (*ESQ: A Journal of the American Renaissance*, 18, IV Quarter 1972, 218–21) is not very helpful. Of more value but requiring qualification is Roland F. Lee's assessment of Emerson's confession to an inability to organize the essay as a work of art ("Emerson's 'Compensation' as Argument and as Art," *New England Quarterly*, 37, Sept. 1964, 291–305).

19. Particularly noteworthy are Albert H. Tricomi's comments on Emerson's epic style ("The Rhetoric of Aspiring Circularity in Emerson's 'Circles,' " *ESQ: A Journal of the American Renaissance*, 18, IV Quarter 1972, 271–83). See also Paul, *Emerson's Angle of Vision*, 98–109; and Elinore Hughes Partridge, "Emerson: A Stylistic Analysis of His Prose" (Diss., Univ. of California at Davis, 1963), 170–84.

20. Jack Null, "Strategies of Imagery in 'Circles,' " *ESQ: A Journal of the American Renaissance*, 18 (IV Quarter 1972), 270.

Chapter III

1. *Freedom and Fate*, 111–22. See also Stuart C. Woodruff, "Emerson's 'Self-Reliance' and 'Experience,'" *Emerson Society Quarterly*, no. 47 (II Quarter 1967), 48–50.

2. Emerson was exposed to geological information from numerous direct and literary sources, including his brother-in-law C. T. Jackson. Of interest is Kenneth Walter Cameron's "Geological Speculation at Emerson's Harvard in 1825," *Emerson Society Quarterly*, no. 16 (III Quarter 1959), 30–43.

3. For Emerson's notions of the west, see Ernest Marchand "Emerson and the Frontier," *American Literature* 3 (May 1931), 149–74; and Michael H. Cowan, *City of the West: Emerson, America, and Urban Metaphor* (New Haven: Yale Univ. Press, 1967), 32–72.

4. Sheldon W. Liebman discusses the importance of balance in Emerson's thought: "Emerson's Transformation in the 1820's," *American Literature*, 40 (May 1968), 133–54.

5. *Crescive*, an unusual word, refers to the capacity for growth. Emerson's use of the word was, I believe, dictated not only by its appropriateness to his view of the expanding self but also by its suggestion of the word *crescent*. My discussion focuses on the latter feature of this word.

6. *Remembrances of Emerson* (New York: International Book, 1903), 15–16. For useful essays on Emerson's views in *Representative Men*, see Perry Miller, "Emersonian Genius and the American Democracy," *New England Quarterly*, 26 (March 1953), 27–44; and Theodore L. Gross, "Under the Shadow of Our Swords: Emerson and the Heroic Ideal," *Bucknell Review*, 17 (March 1969), 22–34.

7. In the essay Emerson develops the expected observations about circles and rotation (e.g., W, IV, 19, 31), the repetitious exegesis of which I am sure the reader will gladly forego, in conjunction with a motif composed of references to centripetal and centrifugal force, inertia, and magnetic fields. The connection between the latter motif and the central image of the explorer is provided by a pun on the word *field*, referring to areas of exploration as well as to those of magnetic attraction.

8. For a discussion of Emerson's views on the railroad, see G. Ferris Cronkhite, "The Transcendental Railroad," *New England Quarterly*, 24 (Sept. 1951), 306–28.

Chapter IV

1. See my *The Writings of Jonathan Edwards: Theme, Motif, and Style* (College Station: Texas A&M Univ. Press, 1975), 55–58, 134–37, 145–49.

2. See Perry Miller, "From Edwards to Emerson," *New England Quarterly*, 13 (Dec. 1940), 589–617.

3. See *Will and the Word*, 67–76. Certain other features of Emerson's Puritan heritage are treated vaguely by Robert C. Pollack, "The Single Vision," in *American Classics Reconsidered: A Christian Appraisal*, ed. Harold C. Gardiner (New York: Scribner's, 1958), 49–53.

4. Emerson suggests the relation between nature and the heart with regard to man's religion by referring to the crab apple tree, although the exact point of transition between them and the motifs under discussion eludes me. "A man bears beliefs as a tree bears apples," Emerson writes, and a man "is transformed into his action, and taketh its nature, which bears its own fruit, like every other tree" (W, VI, 203, 231). Within the fruit of deeds and speech lie the seeds for new growth, and "every seed will grow" (W, VI, 231). But in order to maintain this process, Emerson notes, an element of wildness, of impulse or intuition, is required: "Religion must always be a crab fruit; it cannot be grafted and keep its wild beauty" (W, VI, 214). The trouble with Christianity "in the romantic ages" is that it has become "the grafted or meliorated tree in a crab forest" (W, VI, 206).

5. For discussions of Emerson's ideas about evolution, see Whicher, *Freedom and Fate*, 141–45; Carl F. Strauch, "Emerson's Sacred Science," *PMLA*, 73 (June 1958), 237–50; and Nina Baym, "From Metaphysics to Metaphor: The Image of Water in Emerson and Thoreau," *Studies in Romanticism*, 5 (Summer 1966), 231–43.

6. The mountain image here as elsewhere in the essay is intentional, but I prefer to reserve explication of it and its relation to human character until my discussion of "Fate," in which it is most fully treated and from which its use in this essay derives.

7. Note that, as an exponent of further thought, Emerson's portrait of thought as frozen solidity and of instinct as fiery fluidity is not actually reversed; Emerson is suggesting that the entire process of the intellect (instinct, will, and thought) is similar to the effects of fire on solidity or fact.

8. In a journal entry Emerson wrote: "Hazlitt compares English genius to that of antiquity, calling the former Pan, & says, 'Pan is a

god, and Apollo was no more'" (JMN, VI, 69). Elsewhere he wrote: "We are liberal to the Astors & Vanderbilts & Websters, & allow their barbarous & semi-beast life to pass, though they give none to the Olympian & divine, yet we ought as equitably to reverence Pan in humblebee & cricket" (JMN, IX, 450).

9. This passage is the subject of John Q. Anderson's note entitled "Emerson's 'Horses of Thought,'" *Emerson Society Quarterly*, no. 5 (IV Quarter 1956), 1–2.

10. Throughout the essay Emerson associates the poet with the coming of Spring and with the dawn. Although the traditional meaning of these images applies, Emerson also has in mind the fact that in New England birds return in the Spring and are particularly songful in the early morning.

Chapter V

1. An earlier version of my remarks on Emerson's essay appeared as "The Slender Human Word: Language as Organizing Principle in Emerson's 'Prudence,'" *ESQ: A Journal of the American Renaissance*, 18 (IV Quarter 1972), 249–53.

2. In "Truth and Nature: Emerson's Use of Two Complex Words" (*English Literary History*, 27, March 1960), 71, Paul Lauter writes: "In using two different senses of the same word within a sentence or two, sometimes even within the same sentence, Emerson forces upon the reader's consciousness the relationship implicit among threads of meaning and the significance of those relationships."

3. The earlier passage comes from an 1840 journal entry (JMN, VII, 496).

4. The motif of health, like that of wealth, occurs in Emerson's essays time and again.

5. *Spires of Form*, 187.

6. Paul, *Emerson's Angle of Vision*, 21–22.

7. Although he does not explore the ideas underlying the problem, Sanford Pinsker does note this tension in "Emerson's Anti-Essay: The Dissolving Rhetoric of 'Intellect,'" *ESQ: A Journal of the American Renaissance*, 18 (IV Quarter 1972), 284–87.

8. Throughout "Intellect" Emerson employs wall and prison imagery to suggest the barrier posed by the idea which has become a rigid form.

9. Cf. "God hides the stars in a deluge of light. That is his chosen curtain. So he hides the great truths in the simplicity of the common consciousness" (JMN, V, 76).

10. Cf. "Ignorance seldom *vaults* into knowledge, but passes into it through an intermediate state of obscurity, even as night into day through twilight. All speculative Truths . . . suppose an act of the Will" (Coleridge, *The Friend,* 1:115).

11. Emerson's water imagery in this essay portrays this circular process. See Nina Baym, "From Metaphysics to Metaphor: The Image of Water in Emerson and Thoreau," 231–43.

12. Although Emerson rejected belief in the supernatural, he did recognize its usefulness. See, for instance, John B. Wilson, "Emerson and the 'Rochester Rappings,'" *New England Quarterly,* 41 (June 1968), 248–58; and Stephen S. Conroy, "Emerson and Phrenology," *American Quarterly,* 16 (Summer 1964), 215–17.

13. Of interest is Franklin B. Newman's "Emerson and Buonarroti," *New England Quarterly,* 25 (Dec. 1952), 524–35.

14. Robert L. Haig discusses this reference in "Emerson and the 'Electric Word' of John Hunter," *New England Quarterly,* 28 (Sept. 1955), 394–97.

15. *Confessions,* XIII, 9.

Index